THE AUTHOR

Dr. Giovanni Miegge, famous for his brilliant study *The Virgin Mary: The Roman Catholic Marian Doctrine* is Professor of the History of Christianity at the Waldensian Theological Seminary in Rome. His growing reputation as a European scholar will be enhanced by this remarkable study of Rudolf Bultmann.

GOSPEL AND MYTH
IN THE THOUGHT OF RUDOLF BULTMANN

GOSPEL AND MYTH

IN THE THOUGHT OF RUDOLF BULTMANN

by

GIOVANNI MIEGGE

Professor of Church History
The Waldensian Faculty of Theology, Rome

Translated by
BISHOP STEPHEN NEILL

LUTTERWORTH PRESS
LONDON

First Published 1960

ENGLISH TRANSLATION © 1960 LUTTERWORTH PRESS

This book originally appeared as *L'Evangelo e il Mito nel
Pensiero di Rudolf Bultmann*, Edizioni di Comunità, Milan, 1956

*Printed in Great Britain
by The Camelot Press Ltd., Southampton*

Contents

Translator's Foreword

RATHER more than two years ago my friend Professor Giovanni Miegge sent me a copy of his book, *L'Evangelo e il Mito*. After reading it once, I decided that this was a book that ought to be translated. The writings of Professor Bultmann, and in particular his now famous Essay on the New Testament and Mythology, have let loose a flood of writing in many languages, and a growing series of translations of his works, earlier and later, into English. Most of the expositions have confined themselves in the main to the controversial issue. Professor Miegge has read everything that Professor Bultmann has ever written, and also all the main contributions to the controversy in Germany and elsewhere. With his wide knowledge of the continental theology of this century, he has been able to set the particular controversy in the framework of wider problems of interpretation and of the understanding of the New Testament. I believe that this book may be as enlightening to some other readers as it has been to me.

Naturally I have been faced by some peculiarly difficult problems of translation. In many places I could have saved myself a great deal of trouble by simply lifting renderings from the existing English translations of German works. But it seemed to me that my first duty was to my author, Miegge, and that I ought as far as possible to see Bultmann through his eyes, and not as I might happen to see him myself. I therefore followed a different method. The whole book was first translated with the Italian and German texts before me. Only then did I consult the existing English translations. References to these translations have been given at every point in the footnotes, for the sake of readers who may wish to look up the passages cited in their contexts. If they take the trouble to compare in detail, they will find that my renderings do not differ in many important respects from those available elsewhere, but that following Miegge's own minute care they tend to stick to the German rather more closely than the free and vigorous renderings of some of the English translators.

The one aim of this translation is that it should be understood, even by those who have not had the opportunity to sink themselves deeply in contemporary German theology or in the intricacies of the existentialist philosophy. Professor Bultmann, his philosophic guides, and his critics all avail themselves generously of the liberty required by German scholars to fashion their own vocabulary as they go along. This makes idiomatic translation into any other language extremely difficult. As far as possible I have avoided jargon. But it cannot be completely avoided. "The eschatological event" is not English, and cannot be made to sound like English; but it has become familiarized by use, and perhaps it is best to leave it as it is. At one point a word of explanation is needed. Bultmann makes a distinction, impossible to make in English, between the *historisch*, the thing that merely happens and lies buried in the past, and the *geschichtlich*, the thing that both happens and is significant, and therefore in some sense is always present. I have usually represented this distinction by the words "mere history" and "real history"; this seems to me to come as near as I can get to what Professor Bultmann means.

The translation has had the advantage of being carefully read by Professor Miegge, who has been good enough to agree that it represents with reasonable accuracy his own understanding of the work and witness of Rudolf Bultmann.

S. N.

Introduction

THE PROBLEM

Bultmann's Essay on "demythologizing" the New Testament

IN 1941, when the second world war was at its height, a
small book by Rudolf Bultmann, entitled *Offenbarung und
Heilsgeschehen* ("Revelation and the Event of Redemption"),[1]
was published in Germany in a limited edition owing to the
difficulties prevailing at that moment. The second of the
essays contained in this volume set forth the thesis, which has
since become so famous, of the necessity of "demythologizing"
the New Testament.

The argument of Bultmann, because of the incisive and
radical form in which it was expressed no less than because
of the position that he maintained, set in motion lively echoes
and a certain anxiety in theological circles in Germany. It
immediately gave rise to a discussion in which a number of the
scholars most eminent in the fields of biblical exegesis and
systematic theology took part; but, as a result of the limitations
natural in time of war, the discussion remained restricted to
ecclesiastical circles. The most notable reactions were com-
municated through the spoken word, in gatherings of church-
men, and were then circulated in mimeographed and not in
printed form.[2]

Christians in countries outside Germany had no idea of the
serious problem which the evangelical Churches in Germany
were discussing. All the news which leaked out, and called forth
a mixture of anxiety and admiration, concerned the Church
struggle, which threw the "Confessing Church" into opposition to the totalitarianism of Hitler's régime and led to the

---

[1] These Essays formed the seventh volume of the *Beiträge zur evangelischen
Theologie* (Munich 1941). The title of the second Essay was "Neues Testament
und Mythologie" ("New Testament and Mythology").

[2] I refer to the Essays later published in Vol. I and in part of Vol. II of *Kerygma
und Mythos* (1951 and 1952, ed. Hans Werner Bartsch), in particular those of G.
Harbsmeier, Ernst Lohmeyer, Julius Schniewind, Helmuth Thielicke in Vol. I,
and that of H. Sauter in Vol. II.

imprisonment of a number of Protestant pastors and Roman Catholic priests in the concentration camps maintained by that régime. Very few indeed, if any, outside Germany were aware that, in the midst of conflict and suffering, the Church had shown itself capable of finding the serenity of spirit necessary for the discussion of a grave and fundamental question, which involved difficult problems of historical criticism, of the history of religions and of the interpretation of the most central texts of the Gospels, and which presented a serious challenge to the Christian message as it has been traditionally proclaimed by the Church.

While all this was going on, Rudolf Bultmann published a great Commentary on the Gospel according to St. John,[1] and prepared a *Theology of the New Testament*,[2] a work of immense erudition, such as can be the fruit only of a life entirely devoted to biblical studies, supported by a more than ordinary intelligence and versatility. When the war came to an end, and the cultural contacts which it had interrupted could be resumed, the fame of Bultmann, which was already considerable among those specially interested in the scientific study of the Bible, unexpectedly spread throughout the whole world; and at the same time, as a result of the publication by H. W. Bartsch of the principal relevant documents,[3] Bultmann's argument in favour of "demythologization" of the New Testament became common property.

The learned world tended to regard Bultmann as the greatest living expositor of the New Testament; and the general public, in so far as it is interested in religious affairs, became aware of the emergence of a great controversy, comparable to those

[1] *Das Evangelium des Johannes erklärt von D. Rudolf Bultmann* (Göttingen). The two editions which appeared respectively in 1941 and 1950 are in fact the 10th and 11th editions of the Commentary in the series of critical and exegetical commentaries founded by H. A. Meyer. The earlier commentaries on John in this series were the handiwork of H. A. Meyer himself (1st to 5th editions, between 1834 and 1869) and of Bernhard Weiss (6th to 9th editions, between 1880 and 1902). Each of these was a classic in its time. The commentary of Bultmann differs from its predecessors in the more radically critical position which he upholds, but maintains the profound theological seriousness which has always been a mark of the commentaries in the Meyer series. [E.Tr. in preparation.]

[2] *Theologie des Neuen Testaments* (Tübingen 1948-53, E. Tr. Vol. I, 1948; Vol. II, 1952).

[3] Hans Werner Bartsch: *Kerygma und Mythos: Ein theologisches Gespräch* (Hamburg-Volksdorf, Vol. I, 2nd ed., 1951; Vol. II, 1952).

provoked in the nineteenth century by the publication of Strauss' *Life of Christ* in Germany and the *Vie de Jésus* of Renan in France, and at the beginning of this century by the appearance of the exegetical works of Loisy. From that time on, a steady stream of discussion of the views of Bultmann has continued to spread in many directions, though little has been added to the dimensions of the problem as originally set forth by him. *Entmythologisieren, Entmythologisierung*, "to demythologize", "demythologization" have become a kind of fashionable catchwords. This, of course, affords no justification for refusing to recognize the seriousness of the problem which these words denote.

Faith and Cosmology

The Essay of Bultmann on "The New Testament and Mythology"[1] sprang from a deep concern of its author in the practical domain. This is evident, on a first reading of it, from the straightforward and concise form in which it is set forth, and from a certain simplification not often to be met with in the major writings of this scholar. Bultmann was concerned about preaching and the cure of souls; and, in a wider field, about the contacts between Christianity and the world of culture, and the responsibility of the Christian faith in relation to that world. In the past this sense of responsibility was a major interest and a major concern of liberal Protestantism, as it had been of Roman Catholic modernism. In more recent times it had been somewhat driven into the background by the attitude of the "dialectical theology", which had expressly proclaimed its purpose of maintaining its independence *vis-à-vis* contemporary patterns of thought. In the hands of Karl Barth the master, this principle had created an atmosphere of controversial tension, which itself was of great cultural value; but in the hands of his followers it often took the form of a new and literalistic orthodoxy, which had no contact with wider worlds of thought.

[1] Reprinted on pp. 15-48 of *Kerygma und Mythos*, Vol. I, under the title "Neues Testament und Mythologie: Das Problem der Entmythologisierung der neutestamentlichen Verkündigung" ("New Testament and Mythology: the problem of eliminating the mythological elements from the proclamation of the New Testament"). E. Tr. in *Kerygma and Myth* (1953) pp. 1-44.

Here, in brief outline, is Bultmann's argument: The Christian faith is a mystery; but not in the sense commonly attributed to that term, as though it were a mysterious doctrine beyond or above reason; that may be true of the mystery religions, or of the Gnostic ideas, which were so widely diffused in the dying society of the Mediterranean world shortly before and after the beginning of the Christian era. The Christian faith is a mystery in the sense of a proclamation, a message, in Greek a *Kerygma*.

This term, derived from the language of the court, denotes a communication emanating from the authority of the emperor, the notification of a decision, of the will of that sovereign majesty. In the Christian vocabulary it signifies the proclamation of the saving will of God, mercy offered to sinners, hope offered to the doubtful, the meaning of life revealed to the uncertain—all of these, gifts that demand a capacity for obedience and goodwill rather than an intellect qualified to sound the mysteries of the universe. But this message of salvation was wrapped up in the Gospels in a mythical form, a vehicle which was serviceable though not without its dangers in the period at which the proclamation was first made, but which, to put it mildly, presents a considerable number of problems to the hearer of the present day. It is of course true that there are many men of religious spirit who find no obstacle in this mythical form of the message; they pass quite naturally beyond the veil; the myth is no more than a transparent symbol, through which they grasp without difficulty the unchanging substance of the message of the Gospels. But not all are equally gifted. And, if it is possible to help some to apprehend the message in detachment from its mythical garb, why should we not come to their help?

In the Protestant Churches preaching, teaching and the cure of souls are marked by a lack of precision as to what is really meant. This can only be because the teachers have deliberately chosen to maintain this element of obscurity. Their policy may be defended as prudence in the handling of weaker spirits, as respect for forms of teaching which are consecrated by long use and are dear to the hearts of all. But all too often the impression may be given that the mythical

4

form is essential to the message, that it constitutes part of it, that it is an object of faith, that it must be accepted precisely because it is contrary to all our modern ways of thinking; it is to be accepted as a "mystery" which must be believed, even at the price of the sacrifice of the intellect.

In such cases the difficulty necessarily inherent in the Christian message (the problem of our existence in the sight of God) is complicated by gratuitous and unnecessary difficulties, such as may at times conceal the immediate relevance of the message, and may help to justify modern man in too ready a refusal to take it seriously into consideration. Obviously it is to the interest of the Church to get rid, as far as it possibly can, of those difficulties which are unrelated to the realities of the faith. The problem, as can easily be understood, becomes particularly grave in periods of confusion and of crisis, when the validity of all values is questioned; it cannot be regarded as fortuitous or without significance that it was in the atmosphere of war and of National Socialism that this fresh discussion of the problem developed.

The challenge to which we have drawn attention was not new; indeed there is very little that is new either in what Bultmann set out to do, or in the way in which he has formulated his aims. What was new was the frankness with which the problem was presented to public opinion, both within the Church and outside it, the intellectual rigour with which it was treated, and at the same time the evident desire of its author to remain firmly within the limits of the Christian faith, with his claim that, for all his critical expurgation of the message, he had in fact repristinated the doctrine of justification by faith, that specially characteristic doctrine of Lutheran orthodoxy.

Let us run rapidly through Bultmann's statement of his case.

The picture of the universe that is given in the New Testament is mythological. The world is like a three-storeyed building. In the middle is the earth; above it is heaven, below it is the subterranean world. Heaven is the dwelling-place of God and of the celestial beings, the angels; the lower world is hell, the place of torment. But the earth itself is not simply the scene of natural, everyday events, of forethought and of labour, in which it is possible to reckon with a regular and unchanging order; this

5

earth too is the scene of the action of supernatural forces, of God and of His angels, of Satan and of his demons. These supernatural forces intervene in natural events, in the thoughts, in the will, in the actions of men; miracles are not out of the way occurrences. Man is not master of his own life; demons can "take possession" of him; Satan may suggest evil thoughts to him; but equally God may direct his thoughts and his will, may cause him to see heavenly visions, may enable him to hear his word of command or of consolation, may grant him the supernatural power of his Spirit. History does not follow a smooth and regular course; its direction and its movement are controlled by the supernatural powers. The present "world-order" is subject to the power of Satan, of sin, and of death (all these are regarded as "powers" in the proper sense of that term); it moves rapidly towards its end; moreover, that end is no far distant event; ere long it will culminate in a cosmic catastrophe. Near at hand are the "sorrows" of the last days, the coming of the judge from heaven, the resurrection of the dead, the judgment in which salvation or perdition will be decreed.[1]

The picture is drawn in fine, bold strokes. It includes a number of obvious observations. No educated Christian to-day regards the Ptolemaic pattern of the universe as a necessary part of his faith. But Bultmann introduces other affirmations which do not so immediately command assent. It is not impossible to separate from the concept of a three-storeyed universe the idea of a transcendence of Spirit over spirit, and of a possible relationship between the transcendent Spirit and the finite spirit. Bultmann himself would be the last to deny this, as we shall see more clearly later on. Further, it has to be admitted that from the start the description of the legitimate difficulties of modern man face to face with a "mythical" faith has about it something a little artificial and disquieting. The same impression, in a somewhat aggravated form, is left upon the mind by the next paragraph, in which the more problematic aspects of the ideas of Bultmann are set forth:

The manner in which the salvation-event, which is the special content of the New Testament preaching, is set forth, corresponds to this mythological understanding of the universe. It is affirmed

---

[1] *Kerygma und Mythos* I, p. 15 (E. Tr. pp. 1-2).

in the language of mythology that now the time of the end has come: "When the time was fulfilled", God sent forth His Son. This Son, who is a divine pre-existent being, appears upon earth as a man; his death on the cross, the death of a criminal, makes expiation for the sins of men. His resurrection is the beginning of that cosmic catastrophe, as a result of which death, which was brought into the world by Adam, is annulled; the demonic powers have been deprived of their authority. The Risen One is exalted to heaven, where He sits at the right hand of God. He has been made Lord and King. He will return on the clouds of heaven to perfect the work of salvation; then the resurrection of the dead and the judgment will take place; finally sin, death, and all suffering will be brought to an end. And all this is to take place soon; Paul thinks that he may personally participate in the great event. All who belong to the community of Christ are linked to the Lord by means of baptism and the Lord's Supper; and, unless they behave unworthily of their vocation, are assured of resurrection unto salvation. The believers already have the earnest of salvation, that is the Spirit, who is at work in them, bears witness to them concerning their adoption as sons of God, and guarantees their resurrection.[1]

"All this", adds Bultmann, "is mythological language, and each separate element in it can easily be traced back to the contemporary mythology of Jewish apocalyptic or of the Gnostic myth of redemption." And here is the thesis which the Essay was written to maintain:

To-day, in so far as this message is set forth in mythological phraseology, it has become incredible to the man of our time, since he is convinced that this way of looking at the world is obsolete. So the Christian preacher to-day finds himself confronted by the question whether, in inviting men to believe, he is at the same time requiring their assent to a mythical cosmology which is now out of date. If such assent cannot be demanded, we must consider whether the New Testament proclamation enshrines a truth which is independent of the mythical cosmology. If we are convinced that it does, the task of theology will be to eliminate the mythological elements from the preaching of the Christian faith.[2]

[1] *Kerygma und Mythos* I, pp. 15-16 (E. Tr. p. 2). We have omitted the biblical references in the footnotes, which in any case are obvious.
[2] *ibid.* (E. Tr. p. 3).

Let us now, summarizing Bultmann, go on to consider the way in which he has tried to solve the problem.

It is quite clear that Christian preaching cannot require of modern man that he should accept the mythical cosmology as true. To claim such acceptance would be absurd, since that cosmology as such is not specifically Christian; it is simply the pre-scientific cosmology of an age long gone by; and it would be not merely absurd, it would be impracticable, since clearly man does not invent a view of the world to suit his own particular taste; he receives one, with all the cultural correlates of a particular period which constitutes his historical situation. It is true that it may be possible, under the veil of an ancient cosmology, to rediscover truths the understanding of which had been lost in one period or another of rational criticism; this has been true in relation to the New Testament as elsewhere. But it is not to be supposed that such an ancient cosmology can be arbitrarily brought to life again, out of regard for the values which are supposed to be inherent in it, and which might be lost without its aid.

Thus the expressions in the apostolic tradition "he descended into hell", "he ascended into heaven", can have meaning for us only if we detach them from the spatial significance which is involved if they are taken literally. The same can be said of the belief in spirits and demons, of the belief in the influence of the stars, and of the miracles of the New Testament. If we try to defend the historical character of these miracles by having recourse to scientific explanations, what we are in fact really affirming is that as "miracles" they no longer have any meaning for us. Even the pursuit of the occult to-day dresses itself up in the garb of science.

It is impossible to make use of electric light and of the radio, when sick to take advantage of all the resources of medical and clinical research, and at the same time to believe in the world of spirits and of miracles as we find it set forth in the New Testament. Anyone who claims to be able personally to do so must recognize that, if he presents this as the attitude which is required of Christian believers, he is making Christian preaching incomprehensible and impossible of acceptance in the modern world.[1]

[1] *Kerygma und Mythos* I, p. 18 (E. Tr. p. 5).

8

Similar comment must be made on man's understanding of himself. It is open to modern man to regard himself at one time as a purely natural existent, and at another as pure spirit, inasmuch as in his own inner being he makes a distinction between himself and nature. But in both cases he regards himself as a single self-contained existent—it is impossible for him to regard himself as the sphere of action of forces which are extraneous to himself. In so far as he does entertain such ideas, he exposes himself to the suspicion of schizophrenia. Even though, in the light of biology and psychoanalysis, he recognizes himself to be to a very large extent dependent on forces beyond the limits of his conscious self, he does not imagine himself to be given over to them as their helpless prey. For this reason it is completely impossible for him to accept the New Testament concept of Spirit ($\pi\nu\epsilon\hat{\upsilon}\mu\alpha$) and of the sacraments. If he thinks in terms of biology, he regards the system of natural forces as a closed system, impenetrable by any supernatural powers. If the form of his thought is idealistic, the common Christian concept of "Spirit" and of its action through the sacraments will appear to him vitiated by naturalistic ways of thinking. In either case, the New Testament understanding of death as the judgment passed on the sin of Adam is to him wholly unacceptable. Equally unacceptable is the idea that the penalty of sin can be cancelled through the vicarious death of Christ—an idea which is rooted in ancient sacrificial and mythological concepts; and which, when the attempt is made to translate it into the legal categories of which theology makes use, is exposed to moral objections which are too well known to require enumeration.

The same can be said of the resurrection of Christ, if by that term is meant an historical event, the result of which is the release of a power that can be appropriated by means of the sacraments. To a man who thinks in biological terms the very idea of life after death is absurd. The idealist certainly finds it legitimate and reasonable to imagine a life which is not subject to death, but cannot conceive how such a life should be dependent on the resuscitation of a dead body. As for the New Testament myth of the last things, that is ruled out by the single fact that the coming of Christ, the *parousia*, did not take place, at

least not in the way that was expected. Modern man may
think that the world will one day come to an end; but he
regards that end as an event determined by natural causes and
presumably very distant. In any case it does not enter into his
personal calculations.

> [Further] if the Gnostic way of thinking suggests that the Christ
> who died and rose again was not merely a man but a God-man,
> and that His death and resurrection were not facts related only to
> His individual existence, but a cosmic event in which we are all
> involved, it is only with difficulty that modern man transports
> himself back into this world of thought; and he cannot completely
> make this world his own, since there the self of man is represented
> as a natural existent and the event of redemption as a process
> within nature. From this it follows equally that the concept of a
> Christ Who pre-existed as a heavenly being, and the correspond-
> ing concept of man's own translation to a heavenly world of
> light, in which the self is destined to receive a celestial vesture, a
> spiritual body, are to him not merely inapprehensible by any
> rational process, they are totally meaningless. For he cannot
> understand how it could be that salvation could take the form of
> the attainment of such a condition, or that in it he could reach the
> fulfilment of human life, and of his own authentic character as a
> personal being.[1]

The Necessary Re-interpretation

Such, then, is Bultmann's picture of the difficulties by which
we are confronted—a picture now presented in rough outline,
which will become more precise as we go on. The picture,
furthermore, is prejudiced by a certain inclination towards
simplification, and, as several critics have remarked, by a
tendency to make concessions to "the scientific view of the
world" at a time at which that view itself is in process of
undergoing extensive revision.[2] To this last point Bultmann
has replied effectively that criticism of "the scientific view" has
not tended to restore credit to the "pre-scientific view"; and
that, though at certain levels of culture an anti-scientific state
of mind is fairly widely diffused, and in certain circumstances
can favour the revival of a superstitious credulity, this has not

[1] *Kerygma und Mythos* I, p. 21 (E. Tr. p. 8).
[2] See Karl Barth in *Kerygma und Mythos* I, p. 108 and H. Thielicke *id.* I, p. 184, etc.

ordinarily succeeded in disturbing that view of the world which is commonly accepted by the majority of educated men.[1]

And yet, whatever view we may take of these criticisms, and holding in reserve the possibility of a more precise elucidation of the essential points, it remains true that Bultmann's summary statements do outline for us a complex of problems that cannot be evaded; and the great service that he has rendered has been to set forth these problems with a clarity and a courage such as are not always welcomed in ecclesiastical circles. He himself is not unaware that his Essay has the character of a challenge, indeed one may say of a cry of alarm; and it is possible to imagine that the deliberate intention to give it this character has at certain points hardened the lines and simplified the presentation:

> At this point absolute clarity and integrity are demanded of the theologian and the preacher. This is a duty that they owe to themselves, to the Church, and to those whom they desire to win into the fellowship of the Church. The preacher, in his sermons, must not leave his hearers in any uncertainty as to what he requires or does not require them to believe to be true, in the strict sense of that term. Above all else he must not leave the hearers in any uncertainty as to what he himself has quietly suppressed; and in this regard he is bound to be completely honest also with himself.[2]

But we must not imagine that the problem posed by the mythological integument of the Gospels can be solved by means of accurate discrimination between mythical elements that are to be rejected, and non-mythical elements that are to be retained. Criticism in its infancy attempted to make such a discrimination, and this way has been found to be impracticable. We cannot say that there are mythical elements which are separate or separable from the message; it is the message itself and as a whole which is set forth in mythological garb. The problem therefore must be one not of selection or rejection but of re-interpretation. Here we are at the very heart of the demands put forward by Bultmann. We have reached the idea which renders his attempt particularly interesting, and makes

---

[1] *Kerygma und Mythos* I, p. 18, n.i.   [2] *ibid.*, p. 21 (E. Tr. p. 9).

it impossible that even those whose faith is confident and inflexible in its demands should refuse out of hand to consider it.

To eliminate the mythological means then to re-interpret. But, notes our author, an interpretation of the myth is suggested, and one might go so far as to say is required, by the nature of the myth itself, and by the use which is made of it in the New Testament.

The particular purpose of the myth is not that of providing an objective picture of the world; what finds expression in it is rather man's understanding of his own being in his world. The myth is not to be interpreted in terms of cosmology, but in terms of the understanding of man's being, or better still, existentially. . . . The myth gives expression to man's belief that the origin and purpose of the known and tangible world, in which he lives, are not to be found within that world itself; that on the contrary its origin and its limits lie outside the known and tangible reality; that this reality is constantly invaded and threatened by uncanny (*unheimlich*) powers which are both its source and its limit. The myth further expresses man's awareness that he is not master of his own being, that he is a dependent creature not only within the limits of the known world, but dependent above all on those powers that rule beyond the limits of the known, and that it is precisely in this situation of dependence that he can be set free from the powers of the world that he knows.

So then the myth itself contains the motive for the criticism of itself, that is, of the objectivizing form of representation that it employs. Its special aim is to speak of a transcendent power to which the world and man alike are subject; but that aim is impeded and clouded by the character of the imagery that it uses.

For this reason, what needs to be considered in the mythology of the New Testament is not the objective imagery in which it finds expression, but only that understanding of existence which it is intended to set forth. The question at issue is that of the truth of this understanding; faith affirms that it is true; and faith should not be tied down to the world of mythological representation in which the New Testament moves.[1]

We may add that this kind of re-interpretation is required by the writings of the New Testament themselves; these, so to speak, set the example for their own "demythologization", in

[1] *Kerygma und Mythos* I, pp. 22-3 (E. Tr. p. 10-11).

the liberty and variety with which they make use of the language of myth as an instrument for the expression of truths which themselves are not mythical. The various explanations of the death of Christ, for example, which are given in the apostolic writings and in particular in the Epistles of the apostle Paul, are in many cases objectively irreconcilable with one another. They cease to contradict one another, only if we go behind the form of expression in which they are couched, and try to understand their existential significance. These partial contradictions can be understood in the light of the general observation that the New Testament as a whole is permeated by two different conceptions of man; at one moment he is regarded as a being subject to cosmic determinism; at others he is treated as a will that is challenged to make a decision of its own. Sin is under one aspect destiny, and under another guilt. In the style in which Paul writes, the indicative is frequently translated into a corresponding imperative. Some of the declarations of the New Testament can be made immediately relevant to the man of our day, whereas others remain closed to his understanding. Therefore the affirmations of the New Testament cannot be accepted uncritically, and the New Testament itself in certain parts indicates the ways in which the mythological element can be eliminated from it.[1]

These explanations make it plain that the problem of demythologizing the New Testament is by no means new. It may, indeed, be said to be the thread which runs through the whole of the critical theology of the nineteenth century. But the method followed by that theology is not judged by Bultmann to have been in all respects reliable or adequate. The liberal theology of the beginning of this century believed that it was possible to free the unchanging kernel of the Gospel from the husk of the pictorial forms of Jewish apocalypse in which it had been enclosed, by resolving the message of Jesus into those ethical and religious principles which unquestionably form part of it. We have an outstanding example of this in Harnack's lectures on "The Essence of Christianity". But, in the process, the Gospel was reduced to a complex of timeless and eternal ideas, to an idealistic ethic with a religious motivation, and,

---

[1] See *ibid.*, p. 23 (E. Tr. pp. 11-12).

as Bultmann remarks, the *Kerygma* as *Kerygma* was simply eliminated from it.

> But the New Testament speaks of an event (*Ereignis*) by means of which God has made salvation available to men. It does not proclaim Jesus, in the first place, as a teacher, who uttered certain words of decisive importance, and whom we therefore venerate with unfailing respect, but whose person is in the last analysis a matter of indifference to those who have grasped the significance of his teaching. It does present the person of Jesus as that decisive event in which salvation has drawn near. The Gospel speaks of this person in mythological terms. But does this mean that for that reason we are to set aside the proclamation of his person as mere mythology? That is the problem![1]

Another and more recent attempt is that of the religio-historical school. That school certainly avoids the dissolution of the Gospel into an idealistic ethic with a religious motivation, but it does interpret it in terms of a "mystic concept of religion" which is no less timeless than the other. This too fails to recognize the special character of the Gospel as proclamation (*Kerygma*).[2]

These convergent criticisms indicate the direction in which, according to the thought of Bultmann, a satisfactory process of the elimination of the mythological from the New Testament must be developed. It must not rob the Gospel of its character of proclamation, of decisive word, which challenges man himself to a decision, and in that act of decision bids him come to the knowledge of himself. If we are to eliminate the mythological from the New Testament, this must be done in terms of an existential interpretation, an interpretation that challenges a man to a decision here and now.

The second part of Bultmann's Essay,[3] the freshest and most important part of it, is devoted precisely to working out the broad general lines of an existential interpretation of the Christian message. This is the subject that will principally

[1] *Kerygma und Mythos* I, p. 25 (E. Tr. p. 14).
[2] *ibid.* In an Essay on "The Christology of the New Testament" published in 1933 in the first volume of *Glauben und Verstehen*, Bultmann sets forth through carefully selected examples these two methods of interpretation, personifying them under the names of Johannes Weiss and Wilhelm Bousset.
[3] *Kerygma und Mythos* I, pp. 27-48. "The Process of Demythologizing in Outline: A. The Christian Understanding of Being. B. The Event of Salvation."

occupy us in the pages that are to follow. But, if we are to carry out our task profitably, it may be convenient for the moment to lay aside the Essay on Demythologizing, and to consider at rather greater length the work of Bultmann as interpreter of the New Testament. We shall base our study on writings some of which are earlier, others later and from the scientific point of view more important, than the Essay from which so far we have been quoting. The examples that we shall choose will make it possible for us to study the manner in which Bultmann carries out his re-interpretation of the New Testament writings, not only "in outline", but also more precisely in relation to particular points of interpretation.

I

BULTMANN, INTERPRETER OF THE NEW TESTAMENT

The Forms of the Tradition

RUDOLF BULTMANN is primarily an interpreter of the New Testament. His name, like those of Martin Dibelius and Karl Ludwig Schmidt, is associated with that school which, because of the importance which it attaches to the literary or rather pre-literary forms of the primitive Christian tradition, has come to be known as the school of form-criticism.[1]

At the beginning of the twentieth century, the critical study of the New Testament had reached certain definitive conclusions with regard to the problem of the composition of the Synoptic Gospels, and beyond these it seemed difficult to advance. It was generally recognized that Mark was the first of the Gospels to be written, and that Matthew and Luke were dependent on Mark both for their framework, and for their historical and biographical material; that there had existed an independent source, the *Logia*, made up for the most part of discourses of Jesus; that this source was mainly preserved in Matthew, but that Luke was acquainted with it and made independent use of it; and that there had been another source available to Luke only, to which we are indebted among other things for the incomparable parables of the Good Samaritan and of the Prodigal Son. But the problem of the origin of this traditional material still remains to be faced. If we weigh the evidence really carefully, it is hard to resist the conclusion that, when all this material came to be included in the documents which underlie our canonical Gospels, it had already reached a highly elaborated form. It was then inevitable that the attempt should be made to carry the enquiry back to a stage of development

[1] The pioneer works of this School are, in chronological order: Karl Ludwig Schmidt: *Der Rahmen der Geschichte Jesu* (1919); Martin Dibelius: *Die Formgeschichte des Evangeliums* (1919; 2nd ed. 1933); Rudolf Bultmann: *Die Geschichte der synoptischen Tradition* (1921; 2nd ed. 1931).

16

earlier than that of our Gospels, and of the documents which are supposed to have been used in the composition of them; to go back, as far as that is possible, to the pre-literary stage of the tradition, in fact to the pre-history of the Gospels.

Two methods of enquiry are available to those engaged in such research. In the first place, there is the study of the forms of the individual brief sections which came to be gathered together, though with differences in order, in the basic documents (moral affirmations, anecdotes, controversial encounters, parables, "words of the Lord"); secondly there is the identification, as far as that is possible, of the particular situation in which these were formulated and transmitted, their *Sitz im Leben*, their position in the life and experience of the early Church. This second idea and method had been most profitably used by Hermann Gunkel and his school in the study of another literature, much more extensive and spread over a much longer period of time—that of the Old Testament.

The analysis of the pre-literary forms of the tradition leads to the recognition of the secondary character of many of the episodes into which the sayings and the teachings of Jesus have been inserted. The sayings themselves have been transmitted fairly exactly, in accordance with the principles of the oral transmission of instruction current in the schools of Judaism (*halakha*); but the same exactitude does not prevail in the transmission of those episodes in which Jesus is the chief actor but of which he is not the author; and this also is in accordance with the usage of the edifying literature of Judaism (*haggada*). In many cases the historical or geographical setting of the words (which varies from gospel to gospel) gives the impression of having been simply constructed or invented as a support, in some instances we may even say as a pretext, for the citation of a saying the original context of which has been lost. In many cases this framework is common form, and has no historical or biographical importance. Nevertheless, the saying has been transmitted in association with its setting, and it is difficult to get behind this association, which must be regarded as (relatively) primitive. This unit, composed of saying and narrative setting, is termed by Bultmann "apophthegm", and by Dibelius "paradigm".

It is not our business here to follow up in detail the classification of these forms—it is sufficient to have indicated the method. Moreover, the classification is secondary; it varies from critic to critic; evidently there is much in it that is subjective and provisional. What is more important is to establish the fact that these elements of narrative and teaching had their own independent and fragmentary life in the period of oral transmission, before they were incorporated into the popular literary form of the documents that underlie our Synoptic Gospels. What, then, was their place of origin, the occasion which led to their formulation, and the purpose for which they were transmitted? Unquestionably all this took place in the area of Christian preaching in the broad sense of the term—proclamation to Jews and pagans, catechetical instruction of recent converts, exhortations to the community; in fact, its locus was the primitive Christian *Kerygma*, to use of it a technical term which we have already encountered, and which we shall meet constantly in the course of this discussion.

The Gospels, then, transmit to us elements of the preaching of the first Christian generation in a form not too remote from that of their original formulation. This means that, to reach a satisfactory understanding of them, we must consider them from the point of view of the needs, the problems, and the faith of the primitive community. The Church which transmitted them could not of course fail to leave upon them the imprint of its own faith; it had no wish to avoid doing so; indeed it transmitted them precisely as testimony, as a collection of supporting evidences on which its faith could rest. Now what is the central point of the faith of the primitive Christian community? We have no difficulty in extracting this, not only from the Synoptic Gospels, but also from certain sections in the Epistles of St. Paul which draw on "tradition" (e.g. 1 Cor. 11: 23-30; 15: 3-9), and from the discourses of Peter in the Acts of the Apostles, of which the archaic character is self-evident (Acts 2: 22-24; 3: 13-19, etc.). Here is the primitive faith. Christ, the holy Servant of God, has been crucified by men, but has been vindicated by God in the resurrection; through him salvation is offered, in the rapidly approaching crisis of the ages, to all those who repent. It is in accordance with the

Kerygma that in the Gospel of St. Mark, and in the other three which in this respect follow him, the narrative of the Passion predominates absolutely over everything else. The consistency of this narrative in all essential points makes it plain that here we have to do with a kernel of tradition which had reached fixed form in the very earliest times. The elements of narrative and teaching, of which we have already spoken, came later to be gathered by way of aggregation around this central kernel. In Mark, the purpose is directly that of supplying a historical foundation for the faith of the believer. In Matthew, the prevailing interest is that of Christian instruction. In Luke there is a further historical and biographical interest.

Now this interpretation of the origins of our canonical Gospels already contains within it the two poles of the problem which it is our business to discuss.

On the one side is the *Kerygma*. The phrase has a certain "existential" ring; to put it more exactly, it moves on the plane of existence and decision. Liberal biblical criticism, with its idealist inspiration, understood the Gospels mainly in terms of a humane and brotherly wisdom, which it attempted to detach from its association with ideas of "salvation", and of "the last things", these being regarded as no more than historical accidents. In contrast to this, the religio-historical school, which at the beginning of this century detached itself from the earlier liberal tradition, understood primitive Christianity primarily in terms of a mystic fellowship of worship (the adoration of Christ). Later, the school of form-criticism, taking the primitive Christian *preaching* as the centre of its enquiry, laid stress on the idea that the Gospel is above all else proclamation, message, a word of challenge, demanding the response of self-commitment. This was the period in which Karl Barth and his friends were emphasizing the Word of God as the basic category of the Christian faith. Form-criticism and dialectical theology seemed destined to march hand in hand. This in part explains how it was possible for Barth and Bultmann to collaborate for a time in the same theological movement.

But now we move to another point. The central nucleus of the *Kerygma* was, as we have seen, the proclamation of Christ crucified and risen for the salvation of the world. The school of form-criticism, which had grown up in the atmosphere of Gunkel, Gressmann and Bousset and their researches into the history of religions and into comparative mythology, was accustomed to using without hesitation the word "myth". The "Christ-myth" is the centre of attraction around which the traditional elements of the *Kerygma* came to be organized; the "myth" provides the "framework" for the Gospel of Mark, and still more plainly that for the Gospel of John, in which the Jesus of history is entirely hidden behind the Christ of myth. It is the "myth" which, in the last analysis, gives to the primitive Christian tradition its characteristic and original literary form as *Gospel*, a form which is without parallel in Hellenistic literature.

So then, from the earliest beginnings of the exegetical work of Bultmann, we find clearly identified the two terms of our problem, the *Kerygma* and the myth; the Gospel is proclamation under the forms of myth. Is the association of the one with the other to be regarded as indissoluble? Or can it in fact be dissolved?

This problem has slowly ripened in the mind of Bultmann. That aspect of it, however, which he has suddenly noticed and stressed with the freshness of a new discovery, and with a fervour which is certainly not derived simply from a scholarly interest, is the "existential" aspect of the proclamation of the Gospel. If it is true that the documents are, from start to finish, the expression of the faith of the Church which has transmitted them, it is evident that anyone who wishes to understand them must take his stand within the world of the faith of the Church. The quest of the historical Jesus, with which the liberal critics were so much occupied, is a chimera. The only Christ of history, the only Christ whom we can perceive through the documents of the New Testament, is the Christ of faith. We must, then, approach them not with the cold objectivity of disinterested and neutral students of history, but with a sense of spiritual engagement, with what Kierkegaard called the contemporaneity of faith.

These principles inspired the attempt made by Bultmann, in spite of the limits within which a scholar pledged to the principles and methods of form-criticism must work, to write a biography of Jesus.[1]

To write a life of Jesus, he declares, does not mean to offer the reader a series of interesting observations on the past, nor to conduct him on an archaeological tour. It does mean to lead him to consider Jesus as "a part of that history in which we have our own existence, or rather in which we acquire existence by means of a critical discussion", in "an unending dialogue with history".

> This dialogue does not take place as a conclusion, as a final estimate after we have wrestled with history on the level of mere fact. On the contrary, any real contact with history takes place from the very beginning under the guise of dialogue. . . . But this dialogue is not simply a trick of the subjectivity of the historian; it is the true interrogation of history in which the writer of history challenges his own subjectivity, and is ready to listen to what history has to say, to submit himself to its authority. If we treat history in this way, we do not end up in pure relativity, as though the point of view of the historian himself was the determining factor in the shape of history. For it is precisely here that everything that is relative to the historian, all the presuppositions which have their source in the period at which he lives, in his education, in his attitude as an individual, have to be abandoned, in order that history itself may really be allowed to speak. But history does not speak, if we stop our ears and claim the right to stand as neutrals before it; it speaks only when we come to it with questions that move us to the depths of our being, when we are eager to learn from it. Only when such an attitude towards history is adopted is it possible, is it legitimate, for us to discover whether there is in history anything that can rightly be styled "objective", whether history really has anything to say to us.[2]

Jesus and the Palestinian Community

Bultmann has never, in his later years, abandoned these convictions of his middle period. Taking up again in his *Theology of the New Testament*[3] the problem of the historical figure of

---

[1] R. Bultmann: *Jesus: (Die Unsterblichen)* (Berlin 1926).

[2] *Jesus*, (ed. of 1951) Introduction, p. 8.

[3] *Theologie des Neuen Testaments* pp. 1-32 (E. Tr. pp. 3-32). See also *Primitive Christianity* (E. Tr. 1956), pp. 71-9, 86-93 ff.

Jesus and of his relationship to the beginning of the Christian movement, Bultmann finds reliable evidence of the reality of that historical figure in the conviction, which Jesus was able to inspire in the minds of his disciples, that the eschatological event, the great manifestation of the judgment and mercy of God, was imminent, or rather that it had already begun, and that the decisive sign of this event was his own person. This is to be taken not as meaning that the disciples had yielded to the fascination of the moral qualities of Jesus—this is the pattern that we find repeated with infinite variations in liberal theology from Renan to Johannes Weiss—but in the sense that his message enabled them to feel the urgency of the event and the necessity of coming to a personal decision in relation to it, without ambiguity and without hesitation, in the certainty that a decision in relation to the event, or to the person of Jesus Christ, or to the God who was about to come, was in fact one and the same decision.

The urgency of the decision, however, is not only, and not primarily, an urgency in time; it has also a moral aspect which is fundamental to it. The ethic of Jesus, because understood directly in relation to the coming judgment, takes on a radical form—we have an unforgettable example of this in the Sermon on the Mount; and this radical ethic, presenting itself as pure demand and absolute morality, does in fact disintegrate both the legalism of the Jewish ethic and the promise it makes of well-being as the reward of virtue. It is true, indeed, that Jesus speaks constantly of punishments and rewards; but as the effect of his preaching man, when challenged by the absolute demands of the good, is seen to be without merit, and is forced to recognize his own total inadequacy when judged by the standards of that divine law which demands of him simply but unconditionally the exercise of love—$\dot{a}\gamma\dot{a}\pi\eta$. In the absolute demands which the preaching of Jesus lays upon man, we recognize the unity of the ethical with the eschatological element; the urgency is absolute in the ethical as well as in the temporal sense.

The picture of God presented in the Gospels corresponds to this twofold character of the preaching of Jesus. In his absolute demands God is the judge, the God who is afar off; but in his mercy he is the God who has drawn near to us; and it is in the person, in the message, of Jesus that he has drawn near. He meets man outside the historical dimension of tradition and forms of worship, outside the continuity of the people of Israel in history and in worship. By raising the ethical demand to the absolute level Jesus has reduced the ancient law, the Torah, to merely relative validity, whether it is considered in its ethical and legal aspects, or in its religious and liturgical elements. But just for this reason God encounters every man in his own personal situation in history, in his *je eigene Geschichte*, in the reality of his everyday life. With the unconditional challenge of his demands Jesus confronts every man of every age, in a contemporaneity that can at any time become real. But this is not the timelessness of the universal ideas; it is rather the ever-renewed possibility of an encounter of unconditional seriousness demanding an unconditional decision; the encounter with God who is both God the judge and the God who forgives.

This encounter had been experienced by the disciples of Jesus, and it was for that reason that they called him the Messiah. But what were the ideas of Jesus himself on this subject? This is a difficult problem, constantly relevant, constantly discussed, ever since the publication of Wrede's famous book on the messianic secret of Jesus.[1] But, according to Bultmann's judgment, this problem is irrelevant for faith. The question whether Jesus was conscious of being the Messiah, whether, that is to say, his consciousness of himself and of his relationship to God found expression in the forms of such messianic or mythical and apocalyptic categories as were currently available in his day, is one of those purely historical questions that can never provide the material for an existential decision. The self-consciousness of Jesus is a fact of the past and no more; the concern of faith is limited to the question of what Jesus can be "for me"—the One in whom I encounter God, or more precisely the One in whom God encounters me.

On the level of historical study, Bultmann regards it as impossible to hold that Jesus put forward any claim to be the Messiah. His life was evidently non-messianic, if compared

[1] W. Wrede: *Das Messiasgeheimnis in den Evangelien* (1901).

with what it was taken for granted by his contemporaries that the career of the Messiah must be. But, further, it is impossible to adopt the view generally accepted by the interpreters of the New Testament at the beginning of this century, and to suppose that he deliberately modified the current messianic idea, spiritualizing it in order to make it his own. If he had done so, there would be unmistakable traces of the process in the Gospels, and the writers of the New Testament would not have been reduced to the expedient of explaining his silence by the supposed "messianic secret".

Jesus proclaimed the coming of the Son of man, that Saviour from heaven, who is well known to us from the Jewish apocalypses. But to what extent did he identify himself with the Son of man? To this question, according to Bultmann, no answer can be given. The prophecies of the Passion, in the form in which we have them in the Gospels, are prophecies after the event, and we have no means of ascertaining whether they go back, or in what measure they go back, to Jesus himself. Is it perhaps possible to think that he identified himself with that Messiah whose future coming he proclaimed? It is true that the announcement of the *parousia* appears to be independent of the prophecies of the Passion, and belongs to one of the oldest strata of the tradition, that which Bultmann in his classification of the forms of the tradition designates as "words of the Lord". But these words, too, come to us by way of the tradition of the Church, which understood them in the sense of the fulness of its faith after the resurrection. And what, after all, is the meaning of the word *parousia*? Is it the *coming*, or is it the *coming again*, of the Son of man? In the Gospel tradition, the word is understood in the sense of "coming again"; but in itself it means no more than presence, arrival, and can quite well be understood of the immediately expected arrival of someone other than the one who is speaking. Apart from the faith of the Church, what convincing evidence have we that Jesus ever identified himself with the one who was to come?

We may think that, in all this, Bultmann has been too much under the control of the rigid categories of form-criticism. For, after all, it is no less certain (and this Bultmann himself is ready to admit) that Jesus taught that the closest possible relationship subsisted between his person and the Kingdom that was to come. To take a decision in his favour or against him was equally to decide for or against "him that hath sent me"; in order to follow him his disciples must give up everything, take up their cross, abandon father and mother, be ready to lose even life itself, in the confident assurance that in a higher sense of the word they will find it (Matt. 10: 37-40). The solemn revision of the law set forth in the Sermon on the Mount, with its repeated declaration, "Ye have heard that it was said to them of old time . . . but I say unto you" (Matt. 5: 21-48) is not something that we might expect to hear on the lips of a prophet, however eminent. In the impersonal "it was said", respectful but clear reference is made to the fact that these are commands issued by God; the expression "I say unto you" is not far from the mysterious "I am" of the Fourth Gospel—a phrase which in Hellenistic liturgical usage is tantamount to the affirmation of a divine presence. If the Palestinian Christian community did recognize Jesus as the Messiah, we may suppose that something in his person, in his attitude, in his words suggested this identification. The idea that that community was simply in error in making this identification is a little fanciful, and lacks historical verisimilitude.

However, as Bultmann sees things, the proclamation of Jesus as Messiah is the work not of Jesus himself, but of the Palestinian community. It was that community which set the figure of Jesus in the framework of messianic hopes and apocalyptic expectancy—two spheres which resemble one another but are not identical—and attributed to him the various eschatological titles with which we are familiar: the Messiah (the Anointed One of God); the Servant of God, not necessarily in the sense of the "suffering Servant" of the second Isaiah (ch. 53), but simply in the theocratic sense in which the King of Israel was also the Servant of God; the Son of God, this also in a theocratic and messianic rather than in a theological sense; finally the apocalyptic title Son of man, which signifies simply "man", but "man" in a sense charged with special significance. The Palestinian Church was able to do all this, because it was convinced that in its encounter with Jesus it had been brought to the threshold of the Kingdom of God. This conviction found expression in its belief in the resurrection and in the future return of Jesus (the *parousia*). Belief in the resurrection is the victory of faith over the scandal of the cross, is the interpretation of the cross as one element in the eschatological crisis; it creates the possibility of a theology of the cross. Faith in the risen Jesus projects itself retrospectively on to the Jesus of history and transfigures him. The figure of Jesus, as we meet it in the Gospels, is the product of this retrospective transformation. The question we have to ask about Jesus in the Gospels is not whether this picture of him is "historically" exact, but whether from the spiritual and religious point of view it is authentic. This is the problem of faith; those who like the disciples are aware that in Christ they have "encountered God" will always agree that the figure of Jesus as presented in the Gospels corresponds to the deepest reality of that which Jesus is.

Belief in the resurrection is, then, the all-important factor, the starting-point of faith. As the Church moves outwards from this point, Jesus is brought within the framework of the pre-existing eschatological categories, and becomes Messiah and Son of man. Here we find the origin of all those developments that this understanding of the being of Jesus is destined to undergo in the Hellenistic community and later in Christian theology up till the time of the Council of Nicaea and beyond.

Such are the affirmations of Bultmann; and at this point it is impossible to refrain from a number of comments on them. For there is a startling contrast between the immense importance which Bultmann attributes to faith in the risen Christ, and his constantly repeated observation that the resurrection, as an objective happening in the life of Jesus, is not a fact of "mere history" (*historisch*), and that it is important simply and solely because of what it came to signify in the personal and collective history of the community. In this latter sense it is an event of "real history" (*geschichtlich*). In so far as it can be verified as a faith actually held by the community (but in this sense and no other) it is also a fact of "mere history". On this interpretation, an immense and amazing weight of historical responsibility is made to rest on the little anonymous company of the earliest disciples. What boldness, what spiritual penetration, what creative power! And let it be noted that, apart from Bultmann's assumptions, there is no evidence to justify the attribution of such powers to that company. It is important to observe that everything that is taken away from Jesus—as overpowering and incalculable event—is by sleight of hand in one way or another brought back into the balance, reintroduced into the origins of the Christian phenomenon—by attributing it to the community of the believers. Unquestionably this is a weak point in all the interpretations of the Gospel which aim at reducing Jesus to purely human stature.

But what is Bultmann really after? Is it really his purpose to reduce Jesus to the stature of a man and nothing more? He who was able to call into being in the minds of his disciples a conviction so deep and tenacious that it was able to survive even the shock of his crucifixion; the conviction that with him they had entered into the moment of the great climacteric of the ages; that they had become, and that in their following of him they were, the eschatological community, the community of the last days; he who could do all this was to the disciples, as soon as they had begun in a measure to understand him, no longer simply one of the many, one of that long series of prophets and messengers who from time to time had proclaimed the judgment and the mercy of God. And what he was in their consciousness he must also have been in his own. His attitude of radical independence in relation to the law and to the historic tradition of his people indicates clearly that he was conscious of being not one stage, but *the* stage, the last stage in the transcendent history of the Kingdom of God. His vocation was not the same as that of the prophets who preceded him. It is reasonable to find in this sense of unique vocation the source of the convictions of the Christian community and of its reinterpretation of the figure of the historic Jesus, a re-interpretation which, according to the whole theological thought of Bultmann, corresponds essentially to the reality of what he was.[1]

---

[1] "Certainly the challenge to decision presented by Jesus implies a Christology, but this does not involve speculation about him as a heavenly being, or the construction of a 'Messianic conciousness'; it is simply the rendering explicit of the response to his challenge to decision, of that obedience which recognizes in him the revelation of God" (*Theologie des Neuen Testaments*, p. 44, E. Tr. p. 43). "He

The Hellenistic Community

If the Palestinian community interprets the figure of Jesus in the imagery of the Jewish apocalyptic myth, the Hellenistic community interprets it, so Bultmann tells us, in the categories of the Gnostic myth. The progress of New Testament research has led us increasingly to recognize the importance of the collective and anonymous work of the Hellenistic communities in the early stages of the development of Christianity. In earlier times it was customary to set the great figure of Paul over against the Synoptic tradition, and to regard him as the innovating genius, the second founder of Christianity. Now the tendency is, while recognizing the greatness of his influence, to tone it down a little, and by contrast to recognize all that he himself owed to the Hellenistic communities. Paul himself often refers back to a "tradition" (παράδοσις), which, when its contents are considered, cannot be regarded as purely Palestinian. The greater part of the elements which have been traditionally regarded as "Pauline" in reality go back to this tradition. To it belongs the idea of "mission", centred on the proclamation of the oneness of God as against idolatry (this it had in common with Jewish preaching to non-Jews). Another part of it was the proclamation of the imminence of the judgment, of the resurrection of the dead who are to be judged by Christ; yet another is the use of the adjective *Christos* (the Anointed One, the Messiah) as a proper name, and the understanding of Christian preaching in terms of "the Gospel", the message of salvation which is to be received by faith.

Furthermore, to this tradition belong the Church's understanding of itself as the eschatological community (this is equally Palestinian), but in the new sense that it is the community of the Spirit, the "charismatic community", as being that community which is penetrated through and through by the Spirit of the Risen Christ. Another element in it is the re-interpretation of the history of Israel in terms of the salvation accomplished in Christ, the proclamation of the "true Israel",

himself in his own person is the 'sign of the times'. . . . He, in his own person, signifies the demand for decision, in so far as his summons is the last word of God before the end, and in so far as, being that, it calls men to decision" (*ibid.*, p. 8, E. Tr., p. 9).

28

which is Israel not according to the flesh but according to the Spirit, and is now manifest in the universal Christian community. Another original element in it is the idea of the "new covenant", the typological interpretation of the Old Testament, and the evaluation of the Old Testament in terms of "prophecy" and "morals". But above all what is derived from the Hellenistic community is the new understanding of Christ as *Kyrios*, Lord, and as Son of God, not now in the messianic and theocratic sense, but in terms of mystery and of a doctrine of salvation. With all this is found also the idea of regeneration through the Holy Spirit, but the Holy Spirit working by means of the sacrament of baptism; and the understanding of the Holy Communion, not now as the banquet "of the last days", but as a mysterious rite in which "spirit" is conveyed; and in general the understanding of the Holy Spirit as the soul of the community and as the power that resides in the sacraments and is operative through them.

All this, according to Bultmann, had been developed or at least had been sketched out in broad lines at the moment at which Paul penned his earliest epistles and entered on the stage of that history of which we have written record. Now if we consider the range and importance of this elaboration of Christian thought, and the small period of time within which it must have been accomplished, we are driven to admit that all this cannot have been the original work of the Christian community. The work must have been already to a large extent accomplished in outline, and the categories in which this reinterpretation was expressed must have been there ready to hand. Jewish preaching to non-Jews may have supplied one part of these categories. But our minds will turn most naturally to think of the relationships, subtle and for the most part invisible, which must already have been established between Jewish eschatological ideas and that eastern world, in which spiritual ideas of various origins had been brought together into a kind of unity, which it is convenient to call Gnosticism—a term which is inexact but is reasonably clear.

Was there a pre-Christian Gnosticism? In the opinion of some scholars this question still remains *sub judice*. The Gnostic documents which we possess cannot be dated with any certainty, but are generally later than the rise of Christianity or contemporary with it; it is not easy to be sure how far they are related to pre-Christian ideas, and how far they in their turn have undergone the influence of Christianity. Pre-Christian Gnosticism may be, in reality, nothing more than an unknown something postulated by the science of religions, one of those invisible stars the position of which astronomers determine by calculating the deviations in the movements of neighbouring stars. Adherents of the religio-historical school, however, are in no doubt as to the reality of its existence. "Even though the ideas", writes Bultmann in his commentary on the prologue to the Fourth Gospel,

> have to be worked out in the mass and in detail from documents which are later than the Gospel according to St. John, that the ideas themselves date back to a period prior to the Gospel remains certain beyond a shadow of doubt. This is demonstrated on the one hand by the fact that the basic concepts are everywhere present both in the philosophical and religious literature of the Hellenistic world from the first century A.D. onwards, and in the Christian Gnostic sources. To this we may add the testimony of Ignatius, as well as that of the Odes of Solomon and of the Mand-aean writings. Not only are these writings in agreement. We have to take into account also the fact that the basic Gnostic concept is found in these writings in differentiated, deviating and elabor-ated forms, and that the mythology is often more or less faded and reduced to symbol. All this combines to demonstrate that the basic idea dates back to pre-Christian times. This is confirmed, [as far as the doctrine of the *logos* is concerned], by the fact that pre-Christian Jewish speculation on the subject of Wisdom is itself a variant of the Gnostic myth worked out on the basis of the Jewish faith in God as the Creator, and that Philo on the one side, and the Pauline and deutero-Pauline literature on the other, both presuppose the myth. There can be no doubt that the syncretistic apocalyptic of Judaism has undergone the influence of the Gnostic mythology.[1]

Evidence for this is supplied by the coalescence of the figure of the Son of man in the book of Daniel (where the meaning is simply "the Man") with the Gnostic *Anthropos*, the primitive and ideal man of the Iranian Gnostic tradition, who sums up in

[1] *Das Evangelium des Johannes*, pp. 11-12.

himself all the elect and saves them by becoming man on their behalf.

If, on the other hand, we attempt to determine what kind of Gnosticism is presupposed by the Gospel according to St. John (and consequently by the other New Testament writings which are earlier than that Gospel) we are led to think that the speculation on the plurality of world-orders (aeons), which is characteristic of the Christian Gnosticism of the second century, had not yet been developed (this may be regarded as an amplification and explication of the idea of the *logos*, the mediator between the divine world and the world of men), and that dualism had not yet reached that point at which a necessary consequence of it is the belief that the world is radically evil. But dualism remains substantially the foundation of pre-Christian Gnosticism; its sources can easily be traced in philosophical or religious influences from the Hellenistic world (Neo-Pythagoreanism, Orphic mysteries), in oriental or Egyptian mysteries, or in Iranian dualism.[1] And the same may be said of the mythological figure of the Saviour.

The Gnostic myth, then, offered to the Christian faith in the early days of its development an appropriate framework of concepts and pictorial forms, and Christianity without delay adopted the Gnostic myth as that apt and ready-made channel, through which its own diffusion in the Hellenistic world could most rapidly be accomplished; adopted it, and yet maintained its own independent character. So far from being transformed by Gnosticism, the faith always maintained a controversial tension with it, a tension which was not always equally clear and self-conscious but was always undeniably in existence. Christian faith is giving expression to its controversy with Gnosticism, when it proclaims Christ as the "true" Saviour, the "true" life, the "true" light; but, for the purposes of its controversy, it adopts the language and the categories of Gnostic thought.

This was made possible by the fact that Gnostic thought and early Christianity really had a common range of ideas, or perhaps one should rather say of states of mind, of appreciations of the situation of man in the world. We find in both a

---

[1] *ibid.*, pp. 10-14.

dualistic outlook. In the case of Christian as of Jewish faith, this is coloured by *eschatology*; it is directed towards the future, and involves that negation of the present which is inevitable when thought is controlled by the expectation of a divine act of restoration in time, of the institution of a new world-order, the Kingdom of God. In Gnosticism the dualism is *cosmic*; the vanity of time which returns interminably upon itself is contrasted with the immobile timelessness of eternity, of the world of ideas, of essences, of the divine *pleroma*. But more important than these differences is the idea, which Christian faith shares with Gnosticism, of a transcendent Being, which must become incarnate for the redemption of "the spiritual" (in Gnosticism), of "the elect" (in Paul and John). The identification of the Son of man of Jewish apocalyptic with the Gnostic Saviour was, as we have seen, something that had already to a very large extent taken place in the literature of the later Judaism. But as a result of this identification the Anointed One of God acquires a number of new characteristics. The Gnostic Saviour is the image and reflection of the Highest; he has a cosmic function of the utmost importance as the instrument of creation, as the primordial Man, the *logos*, light, truth and life. When once the identification has been made, the same categories will be employed to give expression to faith's understanding of the Christ.

But was the Gnostic myth really adequate to the expression of the earliest Christian message, and in particular to that eschatological outlook which was characteristic of it in its earliest days? Here we had better cite directly the words of Bultmann himself:

Undoubtedly the Gnostic myth and its categories provided terms in which the eschatological event could be intelligibly presented, as a happening to which the history of Jesus Christ was the necessary introduction, and which is in process of accomplishment in the present; and also made it possible to view both Church and individual in the mighty context of a process leading up to salvation or to perdition. But the problem lies here: is the cosmic event understood simply as a grandiose natural process, which moves forward inexorably without regard to my action, my responsibility, my decisions, and to the mercy of which, for good and ill alike, I am handed over? Is human history to be understood as a series of merely natural happenings, or as genuinely historical occurrence? Is this *Gnosis* simply speculative knowledge, which can co-exist with every other form of knowledge and all human activity, a knowledge the possession of which enables me to face my own destiny after death without grave anxiety? Or is it a genuine understanding of myself, which takes total command of my life, and determines it in its outward expressions and particularly in its actions? Undoubtedly Gnosticism aims at such an understanding of the self, and this expresses itself in the Gnostic consciousness of the possession of liberty (*eleutheria*) and of authority (*exousia*). But the question lies precisely here—is this liberty understood as the liberty of a man who exists responsibly in a genuine historicity, or is it an evasion by man of his own true existence; and consequently—since such evasion is in the last resort impossible—as a pure affirmation without meaning? The question at issue is, in short, whether the paradoxical character of liberty has been recognized.

Moreover, we must ask whether the πνευματικὸς εἶναι, "existence as a spiritual being", is understood simply as a natural quality, or whether it is kept firmly within the category of responsible decision, on the understanding that beside it—and this corresponds to the reality of historical existence—there exists also the possibility of σαρκικὸς εἶναι, "existence as a carnal being". It is only where this twofold possibility is recognized that liberty is truly recognized as liberty. Where this is not the case, we are driven inevitably to the alternative conclusions, on the one hand of asceticism, as a method of demonstrating or of anxiously preserving the spiritual quality of human existence; on the other, of libertinism, whether in this case liberty is simply used as a pretext for self-indulgence, or whether self-indulgence is used to provide a demonstration of the reality of liberty. The failure to recognize the historical character of human existence, together with the non-dialectical interpretation of the possession of liberty and of the Spirit, leads consequentially to the abandonment of the idea of creation; whereas the retention of the idea of the world as creation, together with the idea of "deliverance from the world" through participation in the eschatological event, cannot but become the basis for such a dialectical relationship to the world as is expressed in the ὡς μή of Paul. This failure to recognize the significance of historicity leads on finally to a non-historical interpretation of the idea of συγγενεία and so to a misapprehension of the nature of the fellowship of the Church. Where γνῶσις (knowledge) does not find its own full realization and its authentic manifestation in ἀγάπη, love, it tends to seek its climactic point in ecstasy, which is a means of escape from the reality of history.[1]

In these clear and systematically developed pages, in which Gnosticism is shown to be a form of thought which moves wholly in the realm of the natural, whereas the Gospel is understood in the categories of responsible human existence, we recognize the deepest motive which underlies the demand of Bultmann for the elimination of the mythological element from the New Testament. To this aspect of the problem we shall later have occasion to return.

The dramatic tension within Hellenistic Christianity, in particular in the work of Paul and John, derives from the necessity that was laid upon them, if they were to make their message intelligible to the pagan masses, of translating the historical and eschatological message of the Gospel into the inadequate categories of the Gnostic myth, without falling into the temptation, all too readily presented by the myth, of treating all things simply as the objects of speculative thought. Or do we perhaps encounter here the dramatic tension which exists within Bultmann himself? For those writings on the interpretation and the theology of the New Testament, which appeared at the same time as or later than the famous "Essay on the New Testament and Mythology", are marked by a special quality of personal engagement, which makes them speak with a living voice even through that apparatus of scholarship that entitles them to be regarded as being, from the scientific point of view, some of the most distinguished works on the subject that have appeared in recent years. Both in his commentary on St. John's Gospel (the first edition of which appeared in 1941, the same year as *Offenbarung und Heilsgeschehen*) and even more particularly in his *Theology of the New Testament* (1948-53), Bultmann is engaged at one and the same time in his conflict at point-blank range with the Gnostic myth, and in his enterprise of "demythologizing the message of the

[1] *Theologie des Neuen Testaments*, pp. 181-82 (E. Tr. pp. 182-83). For the ὡς μή of Paul, see 1 Cor. 7: 29-31.

Gospel". Let us consider a few practical examples of his method, taken from his exposition of the writings of Paul and of John.

The Apostle Paul: A New Understanding of the Self

If we have rightly understood this background of the collective elaboration of Christian doctrine carried out by the Hellenistic Christian communities, we shall readily see that there is a very close relationship between the historic situation of St. Paul and his doctrine of "justification by faith". This is the expression of a profound internal revolution, a transformation of the *Daseinsverständnis*, of the apostle's understanding, or rather of his apprehension, of the nature of human existence. This is a "historical" fact, in the sense of personal, existential history (*Geschichte*). It does not belong to the realm of mythology or cosmology. Paul's conversion is not to be understood as a "moral" conversion; it was not the conversion of a "sinner" to holiness of life (as we might be led by Romans 7 to imagine). It involved

> the abandonment of his previous understanding of himself, that is to say, of that which up till that point had been the norm and meaning of his life, the sacrifice of that which until that time had been his pride and joy (Phil. 3: 4-7) . . . it involved obedient submission to the judgment of God, as proclaimed in the cross of Christ, against all human achievement and all human boastfulness. It is thus that his conversion is reflected in his theology.[1]

It is hardly necessary to draw attention to echoes of Kierkegaard and Karl Barth in this attempt to define precisely the nature of Paul's experience.

Paul is not to be regarded as a speculative theologian. The deepest source of all his thinking is simply his status as a believer; his aim is to give clear conceptual expression to that apprehension of reality which is implicit in his faith. His theology is, basically, a doctrine of the being of man.[2] He does not speculate on the natures of Christ, but

> speaks of him as of the One through whom God is accomplishing the salvation of man and of the world. Therefore every proposition about Christ is also a proposition about man and vice versa;

[1] *ibid.*, p. 185 (E. Tr. p. 188).   [2] *ibid.*, p. 187 (E. Tr. p. 191).

35

the Christology of Paul is at the same time a doctrine of salvation.[1]

If, then, we wish to understand Paul's thought in the truth of its historical setting, which is at the same time its unchanging truth, it is necessary first to elucidate the significance of his theology in relation to its understanding of the being of man and of human existence. What then are the categories of the Pauline doctrine of man? How does he understand the being of man, prior to the experience of the revelation of faith, and subsequent to it?

Paul's understanding of man before the coming of faith can be summed up in three well-known terms—σῶμα, σάρξ, ψυχή; body, flesh, soul. These are not to be understood in a dualistic sense (body and soul, matter and spirit); nor are they to be regarded as a trichotomy, a divison of man's being into three parts (body, the feeling soul, the thinking spirit); each of them refers to man in the totality of his being. Man is *body*, in as far as he exists in a relationship to himself, and this may be either normal or abnormal; it may be either harmony or inner schism. He is ψυχή, soul, in so far as he is himself the conscious experiencer of this relationship with himself (in this sense he can also be called πνεῦμα, spirit, if we understand "spirit" here as meaning simply the spirit of man, without reference to the divine Spirit or to the spirit of Christ). Man, then, as ψυχή, soul, is man living as a purposeful being, man as he turns outward from himself to something else (*aus-sein auf etwas*): will and consciousness. In this sense he is also νοῦς, the subject who knows and judges, and συνείδησις, conscience, that is an awareness of his own relationship to himself, and of the demands that that involves.

If we disregard certain secondary categories, this is the essential structure of man's being. But the reality of man as an existent, as it is determined by his actual existence in time and space, is conditioned by the fact that man has chosen a false direction, has "fallen short of his own true being",[2] has turned in the direction of sin. Σῶμα (body) then becomes practically synonymous with σάρξ, flesh, a word which in Paul's use of terms means almost exactly the same as sin;

[1] *Theologie des Neuen Testaments*, p. 188 (E. Tr. p. 191).
[2] *ibid.*, p. 223 (E. Tr. p. 227).

death is the penalty that has been incurred by sin. Because of this false direction, we detect a note of unfavourable judgment in Paul's understanding of the nature of man, as also in his use of the term "the world" (κόσμος), which in itself is neutral. Evidently for the apostle the world is the world of man, and has fallen under the domination of the demonic powers. But in speaking of these, as in his use of the term "the world", the apostle is not swayed by an interest which is primarily cosmological. Death in particular is not the work of Satan, it is "the wages of sin"; and this is an idea centred in his doctrine of man; it is not a mythological concept:

> Paul can, of course, speak in ingenuously mythological terms of the conflict of the demonic powers with Christ, or of his conflict with them (1 Cor. 2: 6-8; 15: 24-26), but in reality he is using these terms only to give expression to an understanding of the nature of existence, at which he has arrived by other means. The demonic powers represent man in the reality of his own inner contradictions and conflicts. . . . Man is not master of his own life . . . The natural man has always taken his decision against God, his true Lord, and has allowed the world—this threatening, tempting world—to become his master.[1]

It is in this way that Bultmann frees Paul's demonology from its mythological colouring.

Under these conditions, the law which was given to man in order that it should be kept (and not only in order to demonstrate to man his inability to keep it) can in the existing reality of man's state do nothing other than convict him of sin. The law is the schoolmaster to lead man to Christ, the only possible way of salvation; not because it produces in him an inner and subjective despair, such as would impel him to cast himself at the foot of the cross (this is the psychological and pietistic interpretation) but because it sets him in a situation which is objectively a situation of despair. That is to say, it sets before him two alternatives; either to remain in sin, or, by attempting to emerge from that situation in his own strength, to fall into "his own righteousness", that is, into the presumption that he can justify himself, which is another form of mistaken understanding of his own existential situation. But man's recognition

[1] ibid., p. 255 (E. Tr. p. 259).

of this desperate situation depends on grace alone; and grace alone offers a way of escape from it.

To turn now to our second question, what is the situation of man in the world of faith and under grace? The divine will expressed in the law is in truth a gracious will. And as the will of God, both in law and grace, is one, so the being of man, in his passage from the sphere of law to that of grace, is also one. This passage does not involve a mysterious transformation of the substance of man, nor a spiritual development of his personality, as in Greek idealism; it does involve the taking of a stand, a change in man's way of understanding his own life; the dawn of a new *Selbstverständnis* (understanding of the self). The historical continuity from the beginning to the end of the process is maintained without any break. The new man is not a "superior Ego", released from the bonds of the flesh, as in the thought of Gnosticism and of the mystery religions; it is the same self of the sinner, but now released from his own inner contradictions, the divided self now brought back to unity; the self which did not understand, and has now attained to an "understanding of itself". "Salvation is simply the fulfilment of man's destiny, of his own inner purpose to attain to life and to self-hood which had been perverted under the dominion of sin".[1] The problem of the nature of salvation is thus set firmly in the realm of the real historical existence of man, and not in that of the cosmogonical speculations of the Gnostic myth.

The new situation on which man enters is that of "justification". In contemporary Jewish thought this term had increasingly a forensic and eschatological reference; in the strict sense, it is the sentence of absolution which will be passed upon man before the judgment seat of the eternal God. Paul in general accepts this interpretation; but he affirms that righteousness, that is the forgiveness made available by divine grace, is imputed to the believer now in this present time. With this transference in time, justification does not lose its eschatological reference, but eschatology is brought within contemporary existence; or rather the life in grace is, quite exactly, "eschatological existence"; and justification, which is not only the condition but also the starting-point of that existence, is the

[1] *Theologie des Neuen Testaments*, p. 266 (E. Tr. p. 268).

"eschatological event". Once again we note the process of transference from the mythological to the historical and existential realm.

Faith in the Death of Christ

Grace is the eschatological event, because it is the act of God in our historical situation; and in the thought of the apostle this act has a name—Jesus Christ; or to be more exact, Christ crucified and risen from the dead. As early as the pre-Pauline tradition (παράδοσις), to which the apostle makes reference, the cross and resurrection of Christ had been understood as the saving act of God in the world, the *Heilsgeschehen*, the eschatological event. Clearly the cross and resurrection cannot be all this in their material reality of an event of mere history, which can be objectively observed and proved. History based on the evidence of documents can establish the fact that Christ was "crucified under Pontius Pilate"; it cannot go on to show that that death was God's saving act on our behalf—indeed it cannot even regard that problem of interpretation as falling within its sphere at all. This can be affirmed only as the result of establishing a certain relationship between the death of Christ and our manner of understanding our life and living it out. It is not "Christ in Himself" but "Christ for us" who can become the saving event. The problem is, then, to understand

> how this event, the death of Christ, can be recognized and experienced by man as the act of the grace of God. For the event can become a compelling and transforming power only when it is understood in terms of encounter with man himself . . . only when its demand to be received as saving event sets man face to face with the necessity of a real decision.[1]

In working out his interpretation of the cross of Christ the apostle is evidently following the lines of the legal and eschatological thought of Judaism. The cross is an expiatory sacrifice (ἱλαστήριον; the cross is here interpreted in the liturgical categories of sacrifice); or it is a vicarious sacrifice (the legal and ritual idea); or it is the ransom-price of man who has

[1] *ibid.*, p. 289 (E. Tr. pp. 294-95).

become the slave of the malevolent powers, the deliverance of man to liberty, his adoption as son of God. But, in fact, in these last phrases, "the categories of the legal and liturgical thought of Judaism are broken through; the death of Christ is not simply a sacrifice which annuls the guilt and the penalty of sin; it is the instrument by which man is set free from the powers of the present world-order—the law, sin, and death".[1]

At this point, in order to give expression to this advance in thought, this understanding of deliverance in ethical and eschatological terms, a further enlargement of the legal and liturgical categories of the thought of Judaism is required, and Paul begins to have recourse to the ideas of the mystery religions and of the Gnostic myth. The death of Christ is represented as though it were the death of a mystery-god, who by his dying and rising again communicates life to those who follow him. But this is only a manner of speaking, an analogy. Let us look closely at a typical passage: "If we be dead with Christ", writes the apostle in Romans 6: 8-9, "we believe that we shall also live with him, knowing that Christ being raised from the dead dieth no more; death hath no more dominion over him." Up to this point the language of Paul is that of the mysticism of the mystery religions; it recalls the mystical identification of the faithful with the god who has died and risen again. But note the unexpected conclusion (vv. 10, 11): "For in that he died, he died unto sin once; but in that he liveth, he liveth unto God. Even so reckon ye yourselves to be dead indeed unto sin, but alive unto God in Christ Jesus our Lord." It becomes clear, from this last sentence, that the analogy drawn from the mysticism of the mysteries is simply a way of expressing a decision which is ethical in character, and results in a new situation of man before God.[2]

To find words in which to express this new situation, Paul has recourse once again to the categories of the Gnostic myth. The idea that "the spiritual" constitute one single body with the Saviour, the Lord of light, is characteristic of Gnostic thought, and Paul simply takes over this Gnostic idea to express his understanding of the Church as "the body of

---

[1] See *Theologie des Neuen Testaments*, p. 292 (E. Tr. pp. 297-98).
[2] See *ibid.*, p. 293 (E. Tr. pp. 297-98).

Christ". The sojourn of the Saviour upon earth was a cosmic event, in which the believers participate through dying and rising again in Christ; and Christ is the head of a new humanity, the "new Adam". But these examples make plain the meaning and the purpose of Paul's recourse to the Gnostic ideas; it is his aim to broaden the legal and liturgical categories of Judaism. There eschatology implied something that is going to happen in the far-distant future; Paul intends it to mean a reality of salvation which is being accomplished in man in his present historical situation.[1]

At this point we are faced by a problem. When the apostle speaks of faith in the death of Christ as the eschatological event, which broadens out into his body which is the Church, he is evidently presupposing acceptance of the reality of the historical existence of Jesus, and of the truth, in the merely historical sense of the word "true", of certain facts in his life to which the apostolic tradition bears witness; it is taken for granted that his life on earth and his resurrection are events that objectively occurred in history. Are we then to conclude that the apostle is thinking of faith in two different and separate ways: first, the faith which consists in the acceptance as true of certain objective facts related to the history of Jesus, or, to be more exact, of certain supernatural events, concerning which it is affirmed that they really took place, that they can be proved and have been proved by historical evidence; secondly, faith as existential assimilation, as self-surrender to grace, the faith in which the death and resurrection of Christ are translated into realities in the life of the believer?

We must recognize, says Bultmann, that such a problem never occurred to the apostle. Between these two orders of thought he did not recognize any difference, any antithesis, any problem. Beyond all doubt he believed in the "historical" reality of the life of Jesus and of the resurrection; and from this level of reality he passes without any break in continuity to his "existential" interpretation. It is, however, essential to note that, if we do draw a distinction between these two planes of thought, it is the second which is absolutely preponderant, and that Paul is not the least interested in the earthly life, the

[1] See *ibid.*, p. 295 (E. Tr. p. 300).

death and the resurrection of Christ on the level of mere history.

Especially is this true of the death of Christ. Paul "can speak of Christ as the Son of God who has loved him, Paul, and given himself for him, only in so far as he has himself renounced his own righteousness, and given up his own 'self' to death". That is to say, he comes to understand who the Crucified *is* only by way of recognition (*Anerkennung*), that is of renunciation, of the abandonment of his own previous understanding of himself, and of the acceptance of that cross which is his own. It is only in this way that the death of Christ is raised to the "cosmic" dimension, to use the terminology of myth; is freed, that is to say, from its contingency as an event in time, and enters into history in the true sense of the term, as the history of personal lives actually lived. This comes about, in so far as the believer bears about in his own body the death of Christ, and thus proclaims it as present in himself; not only so, it becomes present in all those who together constitute the body of Christ.[1] These antitheses are set forth in sharper form in the famous essay on "New Testament and Mythology", as a quotation from that work will show:

> The cross is to be understood as mythological event, if we express it in those forms of pictorial imagery that are used of it in the New Testament: the pre-existent and incarnate Son of God, who as such was sinless, was crucified. He is the victim whose blood atones for sin. . . . This mythological interpretation, in which are combined images derived from sacrifice and from a legalistic theory of satisfaction, is no longer a road that we can follow. But, even within the limits of the New Testament point of view, it does not say what needs to be said. At best it can say no more than that men will receive pardon for the sins that have been committed or are still to be committed in the sense that the punishment for them is remitted; whereas, in plain reality, far more needs to be said, namely that the believer, by means of the cross of Christ, is set free from the power of sin that up till that time has controlled him and from sinfulness itself.

But in the existential interpretation of faith

> the merely historical event of the cross is raised to a cosmic dimension. And precisely inasmuch as the cross is spoken of as

[1] *Theologie des Neuen Testaments*, pp. 296 ff. (E. Tr. p. 303-4).

cosmic event, its significance as an event of true history, the history of personal beings, is thrown into sharp relief, in accordance with that particular way of thinking in which the truly historical event is represented as cosmic, and truly historical relationships are represented as cosmic relationships. For if the cross is the judgment on "the world", by means of which the rulers of this world have been brought to nought (1 Cor. 2:6 ff), it follows directly from this that in the cross judgment has also been passed on us men, who had fallen under the domination of the powers of "this world".

God has permitted the crucifixion of Jesus Christ to take place, and in so doing He has set up the cross on our behalf. To believe in the cross of Christ does not mean to gaze at a mythical series of events which has taken place outside our experience and outside our world, an event which can be objectively discerned, and which God imputes to our advantage. To believe in the cross means to take upon us the cross of Christ as our own cross; it means to allow ourselves to be crucified with Christ. The cross as saving event is not an isolated event which happened to a mythical person, whom we know under the name of Christ; this event has in its significance a "cosmic dimension". And its decisive significance, in the sense that it effects a revolution in history, is summed up in its particular character as eschatological event; this means that it is not simply an event in the past, to which we look back retrospectively; it is the eschatological event in time and beyond time, inasmuch as when understood in its true significance, when understood through faith, it is always present reality.[1]

. . . . .

The cross and the sufferings of Christ are then *present;* and how impossible it is to limit them to the crucifixion, an event in past time, is made plain by the words which a disciple of Paul puts into the mouth of the apostle: "I rejoice in my sufferings on your behalf; and fill up in my body that which is lacking of the sufferings of Christ on behalf of his body, which is the Church" (Col. 1: 24).

Considered as saving event, the cross of Christ is not, then, a mythological happening; it is a truly historical happening, which has its origin in a merely historical event, the crucifixion of Jesus of Nazareth. The true historical significance of this event is that it is the judgment passed upon the world, the judgment

[1] *Neues Testament und Mythologie* in *Kerygma und Mythos* I, p. 42 (E. Tr. pp. 35-36).

passed upon men which sets them free. And in so far as this is true, Christ was crucified "for us". Not in the sense of a theory of "satisfaction", or of vicarious sacrifice. The fact of mere history discloses its significance as the event that brings salvation, not to a mythological interpretation, but to a genuinely historical interpretation; for it is only a truly historical understanding which grasps the meaning of a merely historical happening in terms of the importance of that which it signifies. The mythological form of speech has in reality no other purpose than that of finding expression for the significance of the merely historical event. What the merely historical event of the cross means, when its significance is rightly grasped, is that it has created a new historical situation; the proclamation of the cross as saving event challenges the hearer to make up his mind whether he is willing to make that significance his own, whether, that is, he is willing to be crucified with Christ.[1]

In relation to the incarnation, no less than in relation to the cross, the elements of objectivizing speculation (and that means, in the terminology of Bultmann, the pictorial elements derived from mythology) are only of secondary importance, when contrasted with that aspect of the incarnation in which it is a personal history lived out in actual experience. The affirmation of the pre-existence and of the incarnation of the Son of God—purely mythological expressions—is, according to Bultmann, no part of the *Kerygma* or of the faith, since it has no relevance to the central problem of the faith—the problem of the existential situation of the man, of myself, face to face with God, of that man who must be brought to absolute renunciation of the attempt to establish independently his own value. But, in the

---

[1] *Kerygma und Mythos* I, p. 47 (E. Tr. p. 37). In the Gifford lectures, delivered in 1955 and published under the title *History and Eschatology* (Edinburgh 1957), Bultmann has set forth with perfect lucidity his understanding of history. Historical knowledge is not an objective kind of knowledge, such as is available to us in the natural sciences; it is always an understanding of the self, of the man that I am to-day face to face with the events of the past; and this knowledge involves taking a stand with the whole of my being, a decision which is directed not to the past but to the future; it is, that is to say, an event in my own personal history. But is there really such a thing as the future? It is this that distinguishes the Christian idea of history from any other—the belief that there is a future, that this future has already been realized in Christ, and that to become aware of this realized future is to be delivered from the past. It is this paradoxical attitude which Bultmann designates by the term "eschatological existence". See also the review of *History and Eschatology* by D. M. Mackinnon in *Journal of Theological Studies* IX, Part 1 (April 1958), pp. 205-8.

context of the *Kerygma*, the ideas of pre-existence and incarnation serve to give expression to a decisive fact—that the person and the destiny of Jesus derive neither their cause nor their significance from the concatenation of happenings in this world (*innerweltlichen Geschehens*), but that in them God has acted, and that this action was accomplished "when the time was fulfilled"; these events, then, are the eschatological act of God for the salvation of men, to accomplish which He has given the gift of Christ.

We cannot say that in this sense belief in the incarnation makes it easier to believe in the Crucified; for, the more exalted and more divine the figure of him who was slain, the greater the offence involved in such a faith. In this context belief in the pre-existence of Christ and in his incarnation is no less scandalous and offensive than faith in the Crucified. This aspect of faith comes to specially clear expression in the Gospel of John. But the incarnation of Christ acquires a truly historical dimension ("cosmic", in that sense of the word which has been defined above), in so far as it is reflected in that service (διακονία), which the believers render to one another in brotherly love, and in that mutual self-giving (ἀγάπη), for which Christ himself has given the example, inasmuch as, "being in the form of God . . . he emptied himself, taking the form of a man". Our minds turn to the famous hymn in Philippians 2: 5-11, which, on the view of an increasing number of New Testament scholars, is not to be regarded as a composition of the apostle Paul himself, but as a hymn of the community which Paul quotes as part of that "tradition" which he had himself received.

In the Gnostic myth one of the attributes of the pre-existent redeemer had been his function as the mediator through whom the creation was brought into being. With this is now associated the idea that he is the mediator of salvation. From this we apprehend that creation and salvation are a single unity, and that the love of God which encounters us in the *Kerygma*, the proclamation of the Church, dates back before the beginning of all time.[1]

---

[1] See *Theologie des Neuen Testaments*, p. 300 (E. Tr. p. 305).

The Resurrection

But it is above all when we come to the question of faith in the resurrection of Christ that the "cosmic" and "salvation" aspects assert their absolute predominance over the merely historical aspect. In the crucifixion, what we are dealing with is still a datum of history, in support of which documentary evidence can be adduced, and on which the interpretative faculty of faith can be exercised. As we have seen, the cross of Christ as "saving event" is "not a mythological event, but a truly historical event, the basis for which is to be found in the merely historical event of the crucifixion of Jesus of Nazareth". But the resurrection of Jesus is, according to Bultmann, the kind of historical event of which the authenticity cannot be confirmed by the production of documents. It is true that the New Testament represents the resurrection as an event that has really happened, produces the evidence for it, and regards it as a miracle the truth of which is firmly established, and which can give assured confidence to those who believe in the preaching of the apostles. But this procedure really reverses the true order of the facts. The disciples did not believe in the risen Christ because they had found the sepulchre empty; they proclaimed his resurrection because they had come to believe in him as the Risen One. Belief in the resurrection moves entirely on the level of the "saving event", or, if we prefer so to express it, the historical event to which it is attached is still the actual crucifixion of Jesus Christ. But belief in the resurrection is identical with belief in the significance of the cross as "saving event":

The resurrection is not a mythological event which can be adduced in order to make credible the significance of the cross; this too has to be *believed in,* just in the same way as the significance of the cross has to be accepted by faith. Belief in the resurrection is simply and exactly the same as belief in the cross as "salvation event" (*Heilsereignis*), in the cross as the cross of Christ. It is not possible first to believe in Christ, and on the basis of that faith then to believe in the cross; to believe in Christ means precisely to believe in the cross as the cross of Christ. The cross is not "salvation event" because it is the cross of Christ; on the contrary, it is the cross of Christ because it is "salvation event". Apart from this it is nothing more than the tragic end of a noble man.[1]

In the thought of Paul, the only thing that really matters is the significance of the resurrection in relation to salvation. Christ was "given up for our offences, and raised again for our justification" (Rom. 4: 25). The resurrection of Christ is the eschatological act, by means of which Christ has overcome death, and brought life and immortality to light (2 Tim. 1: 10). Like the death of Christ, the resurrection of Christ has a "cosmic" dimension, in the sense that it is extended to all those who believe in him; as all have died in him, so also all rise together with him (2 Cor. 5: 14 ff.). The resurrection is a reality of the future (1 Cor. 15), but also of the present, and our present participation in the life of the Risen One is revealed in our victorious conflict with the "works of darkness" (Rom. 13: 12-13), in the freedom from sin which we have daily to win (Rom. 6: 11 ff.). The earnest desire of the apostle, who knows himself to be already a sharer in the sufferings of Christ, is that he may "know the power of his resurrection" (Phil. 3: 10).

In particular, the life of the Risen One is made manifest in the proclamation of that life by the Church. The preaching of the apostle is the unfolding of this "ministry of reconciliation", which is nothing other than the saving significance of the death and of the resurrection of Christ (2 Cor. 5: 17 ff.). The "word of reconciliation" which has been entrusted to him makes the cross intelligible as God's act of salvation; it places men at the point of inescapable decision—whether they will or will not understand that they have been crucified with Christ and are risen again with him.

For in the proclamation the eschatological "now" is present reality; this is the acceptable time, according to the word of the prophet Isaiah (2 Cor. 6: 2), the time appointed for that decision through which a man can be saved. It is in the preaching of the apostle itself that the judgment of God upon men is accomplished; he himself, the preacher, is to some "a savour of life unto life", and to others "a savour of death unto death" (2 Cor. 2: 15-16). As in his apostolic labours he "bears about

---

[1] *Kerygma und Mythos* I, p. 46 (E. Tr. p. 41).

47

in his body the death of Christ", so also in his mortal flesh he manifests the life of Christ. He not merely manifests it; in a certain measure he communicates it; "so then death works in us, but life in you" (2 Cor. 4: 10-12).

It is possible, then, to say that "the word of preaching which derives its origin from the event of Easter is itself a part of that eschatological event in which salvation has been brought near".[1] The preaching prolongs that manifestation of the righteousness and of the mercy of God, which was the central significance of the presence of Christ on earth. Through it God continues to encounter men, who, if they will, are capable of understanding him, challenging them with the supreme alternative of salvation or of perdition. In the preaching Christ is present, Christ as the saving act of God. Thus the Church also belongs to the eschatological event; it is not too much to say that it is itself a part of the resurrection of Christ.

From the point of view of the historian, the fact that can be verified is not the physical resurrection of Christ but the faith of the disciples in the resurrection. But for those who can apprehend through faith, this faith is itself nothing less than the resurrection of Christ. We shall not be distorting the thought of Bultmann if we say that though we, the believers of to-day, can no longer see Christ rise from the tomb, this remote event, whether literally historical or not—and for Bultmann it is not an event of mere history—has little importance for us since we do in fact see him arise in the faith of the Church; and through the faith of the Church we receive the invitation to believe in the resurrection—this means, of course, in the resurrection as it is manifest in the potency of life, in the supremely decisive and challenging message delivered by the apostolic Church, and as it ought to be manifest as a present and existing reality in the faith of the believers. Naturally this message is not directed to the evidence of the senses or of reason; it is related only to faith. If we view the matter from a standpoint other than that of faith, the reproduction of the life of Christ in the Church could be considered simply as the extension of an influence, as the survival of a doctrine. It is only faith, and this means not blind faith, but faith which understands

---

[1] *Kerygma und Mythos* I, p. 47 (E. Tr. p. 42).

(*verstehender Glaube*), and which understands because in the presence of the proclamation of the death and resurrection of Christ it opens itself to receive a genuine understanding of itself; it is only such faith that knows that it must be a question of far more than this, and realizes that here we are in the presence of the eschatological proclamation, of the saving act of God, of the risen Christ. These three expressions are after all really synonymous. Our estimate, in short, of the meaning of this survival and of the faith of the disciples is of the same order as that which recognizes in Christ "the Lord":

> The truth of the resurrection of Christ cannot be understood until that faith which acknowledges the Risen One as Lord has sprung up in us. In spite of 1 Corinthians 15: 3-8, the resurrection cannot be regarded as a fact of history which is objectively verifiable . . . But the resurrection can be believed in (and only so can it be believed in) in so far as it, and with it the Risen One Himself, is present in the word of proclamation. Belief in the resurrection of Christ, and the belief that in the word of proclamation Christ Himself, or rather God Himself, speaks (2 Cor. 5: 20), are one and the same thing. Christ is present in the *Kerygma*, not as a great historic personage is present in his work and in its effects in history. What we are here dealing with is not an influence that takes effect in the history of the human spirit, and is fulfilled within the limits of history. What we are concerned with is the fact that an historical personage with his own personal destiny has been raised to the level of the eschatological event. The word which proclaims this itself also belongs to the eschatological event, and challenges the hearer by addressing itself directly to him. This is not the way in which an historical tradition works. If a man accepts the word as directed to himself, as the word which offers to him death and life by means of death, he has believed in the Risen One.[1]

Is this Pauline theology? Is it the theology of Bultmann? In these statements, so different from the purely academic tones of a professor, we may perhaps overhear the accents of a personal confession of faith. Without wishing to anticipate our final judgment on the positions maintained by Bultmann, or to disregard the objections which we still find it necessary to raise against them, it will perhaps be well at this point to stress the

---

[1] *Theologie des Neuen Testaments*, pp. 300-1 (E. Tr., Vol. I, pp. 305-6).

importance of Bultmann's recall to faith in the actual experience of life as being the only form in which the faith can truly be professed. Elimination of mythological elements is not simply a requirement put forward by scholarship, a negative enterprise, an apologetic device put forward as a means of aiding the man of to-day who finds it impossible to believe; it has its positive aspect, in its demand that the faith should be incarnate in the man of to-day as in the men of every other day. Belief in the Crucified and Risen One is the crucified life, which knows the power and the hope of the resurrection. Now here we are moving in the world of Christian faith as it has always been. True Christians in every generation have thought exactly in this way. But they have never supposed that the power of the resurrection can be experienced, except as it comes to us from a supernatural event that really happened; they pass without difficulty from the "merely" historical fact of the resurrection of Christ to the power of his resurrection as it is perpetually renewed in the believer.

Is it possible to separate the two things, as Bultmann would do? Is it possible that faith in the resurrection should become incarnate in a man, unless he believes that on Easter morning Jesus of Nazareth really left the sepulchre empty and appeared before the eyes of his disciples, astonished, doubtful, and reluctant to be persuaded as they were? This is undoubtedly the problem raised by Bultmann's interpretation of the meaning of faith. But it would not be honest to refuse to recognize that, for many who find themselves unable to accept the faith held by the first disciples and by the Church across the centuries, and who nevertheless believe that the resurrection of Christ can have a profound significance which they in no way intend to abandon, the new formulation resulting from Bultmann's removal of the mythological elements may come as a veritable liberation.

The Gospel of John: a Dualism of Decision

In contrast to Paul, John ignores the whole perspective of "sacred history"—the covenant of God with Israel, its replacement by a "new covenant", the election of Israel, the providential guidance exercised by God on behalf of His people. For this reason no use is made in the Fourth Gospel of the proof from prophecy which meets us so frequently in the Synoptic Gospels and in particular in the Gospel according to St. Matthew, nor of the idea of the Church as the people of God. The forms of expression used by John are invariably those of the Gnostic myth; the dualism of the world of light and of the world of darkness, the coming of the heavenly emissary to bring about salvation, the separation of the sons of light who come to the light, i.e. to the Saviour, from the others who remain in the darkness. But the problem is to ascertain "how John interprets this myth, and in what manner the myth is of use to him for the expression of his theological ideas".[1]

Let us take first "the world". The world is darkness, false-hood, slavery, sin and death. But at the same time the world is the world that God created. This fundamental affirmation suffices of itself to exclude the possibility that the Johannine antitheses (light and darkness, life and death, etc.) are intended to express a cosmic and natural dualism (matter and spirit), like that of the Gnostic myth. These antithetical pairs of the Fourth Gospel must be interpreted on the basis of the doctrine of creation, in the light of which alone their true significance can be grasped. Furthermore the contexts in which they are found in the Gospel make plain the ethical, or rather existential, sense in which they are to be understood. Thus the meaning to be attached to the nouns "light" and "darkness" is precisely defined by the verbs "to walk" ($\pi\epsilon\rho\iota\pi\alpha\tau\epsilon\hat{\iota}\nu$) and "to work" ($\dot{\epsilon}\rho\gamma\dot{\alpha}\zeta\epsilon\sigma\theta\alpha\iota$); to walk in the light or in the darkness, to work while it is day (John 8: 12; 12: 35; I John 1: 6-7). The light in which man can walk and work with confidence and with the sense of urgency produced in him by the knowledge that the day is passing on towards the sunsetting

is the illumination in which a man can not merely direct himself towards objects, but can understand himself in his world and find his direction in it. The "true light" ($\tau\dot{o}$ $\phi\hat{\omega}s$ $\tau\dot{o}$ $\dot{\alpha}\lambda\eta\theta\iota\nu\dot{o}\nu$, John 1: 9) is not the brightness of the day, which makes it possible for a man to find his direction in the external world, but the clarification of the nature of existence, in the light of which the meaning of human existence is apprehended, and man attains

---

[1] *Theologie des Neuen Testaments*, p. 360 (E. Tr. Vol. II, p. 13).

to such an understanding of himself as discloses to him his "way", guides him in all that he does, and gives him illumination and assurance.[1]

These expressions are not to be taken as implying simply a structure of thought. They acquire content and a particular meaning, which must be grasped at the outset if we are to understand what is implied in the "understanding of the self" in the sense which Bultmann attributes to that term, and which we shall encounter later on:

If the creation is a revelation of God and if the Word (the *logos*) is active in the created universe as light, this means that the possibility of a true understanding of himself is offered to man on condition that he is willing to recognize his own creatureliness. The "darkness", then, means that man refuses to accept that which is offered to him, and that . . . instead of recognizing his creatureliness, he attributes to himself such sovereign independence (*Selbstherrlichkeit*) as is the prerogative of the Creator alone.[2]

Nothing is to be gained by enquiring as to the origin of the "darkness", and in point of fact John does not have recourse to a myth in order to explain it:

The possibility of darkness, i.e. of the false understanding of the self, is given together with the possibility of the light, i.e. of the true understanding of oneself. . . . It is only through the existence of the light that the darkness can exist. Darkness is nothing but the closing of ourselves against the light, and that is equivalent to severing ourselves from the origin of our being, in which alone we are granted the possibility of enlightenment as to the nature of existence. Inasmuch as the world closes itself against the light, it is in rebellion against God, it takes up an attitude of self-sufficiency *vis-à-vis* the Creator—that is, it attempts to do so, and imagines that it can really do so.

Thus, inasmuch as it is in darkness, the world is also living in the lie. For it is this illusion about the self, and not evil conduct, which is the lie; but, conversely, this is not the illusion of pure error; it is the illusion of a false understanding of the self, in which all evil conduct has its origin, and which exists prior to all individual manifestations of evil conduct; the illusion of an

[1] *Theologie des Neuen Testaments*, p. 364 (E. Tr. Vol. II, pp. 17-18).
[2] *ibid.*, p. 364 (E. Tr. Vol. II, p. 18).

understanding of the self which in itself constitutes rebellion against God and against the truth.[1]

In conclusion,

the concepts "light, truth, life and freedom" mutually throw light upon one another, as do the contrasting concepts "darkness, falsehood, death and slavery". These all derive their significance from the search for the reality of human existence—of life, ζωή, regarded as ζωὴ αἰώνιος—and they indicate the two possibilities that lie before human existence, according as it takes its starting-point in God or in man. They imply that it is only in the recognition of his own creatureliness that man can attain to the true understanding of himself; this is the light that lightens his way; only in this recognition can he become aware of the truth, and of that true reality which is disclosed to him in the revelation of God; only so can he escape the delusion that he can base his own reality on a world of his own making which is in rebellion against God. Only through this recognition does he obtain deliverance from the apparent reality, which in fact is darkness, falsehood, slavery and death; only in such freedom does he attain life, inasmuch as now he is living from the only true source of his being. Man is brought face to face with the decision for or against God—or rather he was. Now he has been brought face to face with this decision in a new way, as a result of the revelation of God in Jesus. The cosmological dualism of Gnosticism has become in John a dualism of decision.[2]

It is in the light of this dualism of decision that we are to understand the Johannine affirmations concerning the elect and the reprobate. The antithetical categories in which men are divided—those who are of God, those who are of the devil (ἐκ τοῦ Θεοῦ, ἐκ τοῦ διαβόλου, John 8: 44; 1 John 3: 8, 10); from, or of, the truth, from, or of, the world (ἐκ τῆς ἀληθείας, 1 John 3: 19; ἐκ τούτου τοῦ κόσμου, John 8: 23; 15: 19); from below or from above (ἐκ τῶν ἄνω, ἐκ τῶν κάτω, John 8: 23) may easily suggest to our minds the Gnostic classification of the spiritual, the "soulish", and the material. But, on the Gnostic view, men are thus divided by their natural constitution, whereas such an interpretation in terms of nature would misrepresent the teaching of the Gospel of

[1] ibid., p. 365 (E. Tr. Vol. II, p. 18).
[2] ibid., p. 367 (E. Tr. Vol. II, pp. 20-21).

John. This interpretation is excluded by John's doctrine that every man is brought face to face with the decision of faith, and it is only in relation to the decision of faith that the antithetical terms acquire their meaning. In John as in Paul,

> the formulations which have about them a ring of predestination mean simply that the decision of faith is not a choice between two possibilities within our world, and that it does not arise from impulses that are active within the limits of this world. They affirm that in the presence of God the believer cannot take his stand upon his own faith. His confidence is at no time in himself, but only and always in God. But, if faith involves giving up the affirmation of the self, the believer is bound to think of his faith not as a free act determined by his own intentions, but simply as God's working upon him.[1]

It is in this way, and in no other, that the affirmation of Jesus in the Fourth Gospel that none come unto him except those who have been given him by the Father is to be interpreted. This interpretation of predestination in John clearly follows the same lines as the re-interpretation of the doctrine of the pre-existence of the Son of man in terms of the existential decisions that man is called upon to make.[2]

The Word Made Flesh

In this world of darkness, of falsehood and of death, light and truth and life have appeared; the Son of God has come. Once again we meet the pictorial language of myth; but what is its meaning in the Gospel of John?

In the first place it is to be noted that the stress falls not so much on the person of the One who has come as on the fact of his coming. The manifestation of Christ is a "being sent" (e.g. John 3: 17; 4: 34; 17: 3, 21), and this is balanced by a "going away" (John 7: 33; 16: 7, 10). His coming is a journey through this world; it is not a phenomenon that can be understood in terms of this world alone.[3]

Following upon this, it is to be noted that the sending of the Son is the act of the love of the Father towards the world

[1] *Theologie des Neuen Testaments*, pp. 369-70 (E. Tr. p. 23).
[2] See above p. 45.
[3] See *Theologie des Neuen Testaments* pp. 380-81 (E. Tr. Vol. II, pp. 33-35).

(1 John 4: 9); in his coming the love of the Father has become manifest, φανερός; we may say that it has become an observable phenomenon for those, or rather in those, who receive the love of God.[1]

The purpose for which the Son has come is "to bear witness to the truth", that is to say, to the love of God manifest in him. The two expressions are synonymous; the person and the word of Jesus fulfil the same function and are of equal importance.

Now the forms in which the Gospel of John describes this manifestation of the love of God as an observable reality on earth are clearly borrowed either from the Gnostic myth (Jesus is the Saviour from heaven), or from the Jewish and primitive Christian tradition, that is from the mythological forms of apocalyptic (even in the Fourth Gospel, though only in a secondary way, Jesus is the Messiah, the King of Israel, the Son of God in the theocratic sense of the word, the Son of man).[2]

In these titles, from whatever source they may have been drawn, the Fourth Gospel gives expression to the conviction that the coming of Jesus is the eschatological event.[3]

In the Gospel of John the eschatological event is brought more radically on to the plane of history, is more completely stripped of its mythological trappings, than in Paul. It is especially important to observe that the "judgment" is not regarded as postponed till the end of the times, but is accomplished in the present, and is accomplished in relation to the presence of Jesus in the world; the attitude that men take up towards him *is* the judgment, that *krisis* of the world, which takes effect in the separation of those who believe in him and come to him from those who do not believe and remain in darkness. He who believes does not enter into judgment; he who does not believe has been judged already; evidence for this is to be found in the conversation of Jesus with Nicodemus (John 3: 16-20).[4]

---

[1] *ibid.*, p. 382 (E. Tr. Vol. II, p. 35).

[2] These points of contact with the Palestinian tradition are one of the puzzling features in the Johannine problem, and for this reason, if for no other, they deserve to be mentioned here.

[3] See *Theologie des Neuen Testaments*, pp. 382-4 (E. Tr. Vol. II, pp. 36-37).

[4] See *ibid.*, p. 386 (E. Tr. Vol. II, pp. 39-40).

The paradoxical character of the incarnation is strongly stressed in the Fourth Gospel, and precisely in controversy with that Gnosticism from which the writer has borrowed those pictorial forms of expression that he uses. As he sees it, the incarnation of the Son of God is not a natural or cosmic process. The Gnostic Saviour liberates those souls which by their spiritual, light-filled nature are akin to him; but John is not aware of, or perhaps rather rejects, that Gnostic idea of *physis*, nature, which implies the pre-existence of souls and deplores their present condition as prisoners in the material and non-spiritual world—we have already seen in what sense Bultmann interprets the ideas of pre-existence and of predestination in Paul and in John. What Jesus communicates to men are not the magical formulae and rites of initiation current in Gnosticism; what he teaches is not the secret knowledge concerning the nature of the world that is offered in a Gnostic revelation.

This is not all. The paradox attains its climax in the clearly anti-docetic tendency of the Johannine writings. The body of Jesus is not, as in the Gnostic tradition, the mere appearance of a body, a spiritual body. Jesus does not become incarnate in an abstract and hardly definable "human nature"; he becomes incarnate in one definite man, Jesus of Nazareth, a real man of humble condition, whose father, mother, brothers and sisters are well-known to all (John does not refer to the miraculous birth of Jesus and does not mention Bethlehem); a man who presents no evidence, and indeed not the slightest appearance, of divinity. The incarnation in the thought of John is paradox and offence. Jesus is not a transparent veil, through which the divine nature can be seen. He is not a θεῖος ἀνήρ, a man of more than human powers according to the Greek idea (though traits of this kind do emerge here and there in the Fourth Gospel), a divine man, whose radiant being communicates directly the knowledge of the truth. Everything about him is enigma and offence. His miracles of healing draw down hostility and persecution on those who have been miraculously healed. His words are misunderstood. His claim to be "equal with God" is regarded as a crime and brings about his death. When he speaks of himself as the bread of life, the people find this word difficult of acceptance (John 6: 60).

We may say that John, in his presentation of the work of Jesus . . . has taken up again in an original way the theory of the "messianic secret", which is familiar to us especially in the Gospel of Mark, and has carried it to a deeper level. The figure of Jesus is wrapped in mystery, although he proclaims openly who he is and what claims he makes. Although he proclaims it? On the contrary, precisely because he proclaims it. For, as far as the world is concerned, it is just the complete publicity of his work that makes of him the hidden Messiah; not because he conceals anything or commands that it be kept secret, but because the world, although it has eyes to see, does not see.[1]

"His work as a whole is both revelation and offence." And naturally, this is more evident in the cross than anywhere else.

In the passion of Jesus the meaning of his "being sent" is completely fulfilled. And in so far as this is understood, accepted, and taken upon him as the fulfilment of the task which has been laid upon him by the Father, the hour of the cross is the hour in which he is lifted up, in which he is glorified. When considered from the point of view of this fulfilment, the whole activity of the man Jesus is a revelation of δόξα, of the glory of God. In studying the Gospel of Mark we are able to grasp the historic process as a result of which the life of Jesus, which in itself was not messianic, was retrospectively interpreted in messianic categories; from the Gospel of John we can learn that this process was objectively justifiable as the explanation of something that was really there. The evangelist expresses this in the prayer which he ascribes to Jesus . . . . "Father, glorify thy name" (πάτερ, δόξασόν σου τὸ ὄνομα), and in the voice from heaven which replies to this prayer, "I have glorified it, and will glorify it again" (ἐδόξασα καὶ πάλιν δοξάσω, John 12: 28). The glorification of the name of God, which begins with the crucifixion of Jesus interpreted as his "lifting up", and the glorification of the name of God through the activity of Jesus upon earth, therefore constitute a unity. The one cannot exist without the other; the one takes place only by means of the other. But the glorification of the name of God is at the same time the glorification of Jesus himself, and to the prayer "Father, glorify thy name" (πάτερ, δόξασόν σου τὸ ὄνομα) corresponds the other prayer, "Father, the hour is come; glorify thy Son" (πάτερ, ἐλήλυθεν ἡ ὥρα, δόξασόν σου τὸν υἱόν, John 17: 1). And since the reason for this petition is "that the

---

[1] *Theologie des Neuen Testaments*, p. 394 (E. Tr. Vol. II, pp. 47-48).

Son may glorify thee" (ἵνα ὁ υἱός δοξάσῃ σέ), the identity of the glory of God and of the glory of Jesus is once again made evident.[1]

In this elevation to glory by means of the cross, the resurrection has no particular significance. The appearances of the risen Jesus, which the evangelist unquestionably regarded as objectively real, are, like the miracles of Jesus, σημεῖα, signs and nothing else; they make it possible to apprehend the victory of Jesus over the world. But, in so far as they are events which actually happened, they are placed on the same level as the visible miracles, and share in that covert depreciation of the merely miraculous which is characteristic of the Fourth Gospel. They are not necessary to faith; they are no more than a concession to human weakness. If we disregard the appendix (ch. 21), and the two concluding verses (30-31) of chapter 20 which are a conclusion added by the final editor, the last words of the Gospel are the words of Jesus to Thomas: "Because thou hast seen me thou hast believed. Blessed are they that have not seen, and yet have believed" (John 20: 29).[2]

The relationship with Christ on which the believer enters is, then, certainly a relationship with the glorified Christ; but not in the sense of a relationship to a heavenly figure, who like the Gnostic Saviour has laid aside the mantle of human and earthly existence. On the contrary, the glorified Christ is at the same time the earthly Christ, the man Jesus. The glorified Christ, ὁ δοξασθείς, is none other than the Word who became flesh, ὁ σάρξ γενόμενος. In other words, the earthly life of Jesus has not become a fragment of the historic past; it remains perpetually present. The historic figure of Jesus, his human history, retains its significance as the revelation of his glory, and therewith of the glory of God. In the fullest sense of the term, it is the eschatological event.

Existence in the Eschatological Dimension

Faith is the knowledge, the vision, of the glory of the incarnate and crucified Christ. But this is not mystical vision, direct and immediate; it remains linked to the paradox of the Word made

---

[1] *Theologie des Neuen Testaments*, p. 395 (E. Tr. Vol. II, p. 48).
[2] *ibid.*, p. 404 (E. Tr. Vol. II, p. 57).

flesh. When, during the discourses at the Last Supper, Philip says to Jesus, "Show us the Father, and it sufficeth us", Jesus answers, "He that hath seen me hath seen the Father"; but he immediately adds, "The words that I speak unto you, I speak not of myself; but the Father abiding in me doeth his works" (John 14: 10). The word and the person of Jesus are identified, for he is the Word made flesh; and so to believe in him and to hear his word are synonymous expressions.

Faith is victory over the offence of the Word who has been made flesh and has been rejected by the world; it is decision on behalf of God and against the world, a decision demanded not by impulses operating within the limits of this world, but by the encounter with God revealed in Christ. Therefore it must not be in any way confused with acceptance of a dualistic understanding of the universe; on the contrary, it is a "decision against", which takes place in a dualism of decision; it is not the recognition of a dualism which naturally exists; it means taking a stand on the basis of a dualism of choice.

Faith means entrance upon "eschatological existence", in which the believers are made partakers of the glory of Christ; this conveys to them the gifts of "knowledge" and of "liberty", in virtue of which they are enabled to keep the commandments, or rather the new commandment of love, the countersign of which is peace and joy.[1]

The eschatological existence of faith is described as "abiding" (μένειν) "in him and he in us" (John 15: 4-9). But this too is not to be understood in terms of a mystical relationship, as is clear from the equivalent expression: "If ye abide in me and my words abide in you" (John 15: 7). To abide in him means exactly the same as to keep his words. In fact, "abiding in him" is a form of loyalty comparable to friendship: "I have called you friends" (John 15: 15); here however Jesus lays stress on the fact that this expression cannot be reversed: "Ye have not chosen me, but I have chosen you" (John 15: 16); the clearest expression of this relationship is prayer "in his name" (John 16: 24), prayer which characteristically has the double significance of nearness and of distance.

In the loyalty of friendship, in this mutual indwelling, the

---

[1] *ibid.*, pp. 425, 429 (E. Tr. Vol. II, pp. 77, 83).

believer receives the assurance that his prayer, offered in the name of Jesus, is heard. But,

> in order to exclude a mythological interpretation in the sense that the glorified Jesus intervenes as intercessor between God and man, he adds expressly, "I say not that I will pray the Father for you; for the Father himself loveth you, because ye have loved me" (John 16: 26-27).[1]

Eschatological existence is characterized by the possession of the Spirit. Spirit is, according to John, the power that makes possible the knowledge and the proclamation of the Word in the community. He is "the Spirit of truth", who calls to remembrance and teaches (John 16: 13-14). He does not teach anything that is new, but he sets in a new light that which Jesus had said and done; not in the sense that the teaching of Jesus is "quantitatively incomplete", but in the sense that it is "essentially open in the direction of the future" (*Unabgeschlossenheit*).[2] The Spirit bears witness of him (John 15: 26); he adds persuasive force to the preaching of the Church, in particular "convincing the world of sin" (John 16: 8). And he is the fountain-head of that "love" which binds together those who are members of the Church.

The Church is the community of believers, which although it exists in the world has its real being in an "eschatological dimension". The Johannine understanding of the Church is set forth not in phrases or images derived from the sacred history of Israel (the people of God, the people of the covenant and of the promise) but in those which are typical of the Gnostic tradition. The Church is, in a certain sense, a fellowship of the initiated, the community of the sons of light, who have "come" to Christ, and "belong" to him, that is, to the Father. We may say that they constitute an "invisible Church". But the characteristic idea of the Church as the Body of Christ (σῶμα Χριστοῦ), of which Paul makes such extensive use, is not found in this Gospel. The faithful are referred to as "the disciples" (μαθηταί), as "friends" (φίλοι), as "his own" (ἴδιοι). Negatively, they are "not of this world" (John 17: 14); positively, their life is an "eschatological existence", a life free and separate from

---

[1] *Theologie des Neuen Testaments*, p. 433 (E. Tr. Vol. II, pp. 86-87).
[2] *ibid.*, p. 435 (E. Tr. Vol. II, p. 89).

the world and from sin, based on their relationship with Jesus, the Revealer of the love of the Father. This life is manifest in their "unity" with him who is the Shepherd, the true Vine of which they are the branches (John 10: 11; 15: 1). In other words, the unity is the unity of faith, which is manifest not in the constraint of a common discipline or in asceticism, but in the fact of "being moved by that Spirit which dwells within it, as the power which makes possible both knowledge and the proclamation of the Word".[1]

Such, in broad outline, is the interpretation of the message of the Gospel which Bultmann offers. For the purpose of this book it is impossible, and in any case it is unnecessary, to discuss in detail its validity as interpretation of the New Testament. We must, however, remember that this is the field of Bultmann's special competence. He is a master of his art, and particularly in his delineation of the apostolic message, in its relation to and in its contrasts with the Gnostic myth, he has made a contribution of the highest possible importance to our understanding of Christian origins and to the interpretation of the New Testament.

But Bultmann's criticisms of the Gnostic myth are accompanied step by step by the attempt to translate the apostolic *Kerygma* into terms of an existentialist philosophy. The two together constitute, in its negative and its positive aspect, the process of "translating" the message of the Gospel into non-mythological terms.

This attempt raises the problem of whether or how far such a translation is possible, without either dissolving the Gospel into a philosophy or misunderstanding the conditions imposed by existentialism on thought and its limitations as a philosophy. In short, we are face to face with the problem of the relationship between existentialism and theology in the thought of Bultmann.

[1] *ibid.*, p. 439 (E. Tr. Vol. II, p. 92). For the idea of "eschatological existence", see Bultmann, *History and Eschatology* (Edinburgh 1957) pp. 138 ff. Bultmann's ideas are not unrelated, in the field of biblical exegesis, to C. H. Dodd's "realized eschatology", and in the field of philosophy to the understanding of history set forth by R. G. Collingwood, Dilthey and Croce; see p. 169, after the reference to Heidegger and Dilthey.

2

EXISTENTIALISM AND THEOLOGY

A Common Problem, Divergent Solutions

IT is not necessary to spill much ink in order to demonstrate the affinity which exists between the formulation of problems current in the existentialist philosophy in practically all its ramifications, and that to be found in the New Testament; and hence the real possibility of translating the language of the New Testament into the ideas and the forms of a philosophy of existence. This affinity, and the possibilities that it opens up, derive evidently from the fact that the existentialist philosophy is simply a secularized form of what was originally Christian thought (that of Kierkegaard); in consequence it takes for granted that understanding of the self which is peculiar to Christianity; we may go further and say, peculiar to Christianity in its Pauline and Reformation forms. Existentialism has, however, severed itself from Christian faith, and aims at rising higher by substituting the clarity of a philosophy for the ambiguities of religion. But Bultmann has initially no difficulty in translating the language of Paul into the dialect of existentialism; indeed the problem of translation hardly arises.

We find, then, that "the world", in the New Testament as in existentialism, is the domain of the impermanent and of the transitory; time which always passes away and disappears; death which is always imminent; and this determination of existence is not to be understood, as in Gnosticism, as a cosmic necessity connected with the material nature of the world; it is regarded as a moral fatality, as a part of the structure of man as he actually is, as sin. Under the aspect of transitoriness the world is the world of "the flesh"; and, as we have already seen, this term is not to be taken in a biological sense; it does not convey an ascetic condemnation of man's emotional life, or of his sexuality, but indicates simply the impermanent and transitory character of the world; "All flesh is grass, and all the goodliness thereof is as the flower of the field", sings the

Second Isaiah (40: 6). But this world of impermanence, of transitoriness, of death, is also the only visible, measurable world, the only world which is available to man. It is the only world in which man can seek for a point of rest, for a security which, however, is always precarious. As a result his whole life is absorbed by cares and anxieties (μεριμνᾶν, says St. Paul, using a verb which very well expresses what is meant by the "Anxiety" or "Dread" of the existentialists, 1 Cor. 7: 32 ff.). But in so far as he follows his natural impulse "to put his trust in the flesh", even this ephemeral world may become the ground of his "boastfulness", of his "glorying" (καυχᾶται; Phil. 3: 4; 2 Cor. 11: 18).

But the confidence and the boasting are ill-placed. They are not well-matched to

the situation of man as it really is; for his situation is not one of security. It is just in this way that man loses his life, his own true existence, and falls under the domination of that very sphere which he had intended to bring under his control, and from which he had hoped to win security for himself. It is just this attitude that gives to the world, which man could have possessed as the world of God's creation, its character as "this world", the world in opposition to God. It is just this attitude which releases into existence those "powers", by which man is dominated, and which precisely because they stand in relation to him as "powers", can rightly be spoken of as mythological forces. (Such expressions as "the spirit of the times" or "the spirit of technology" come readily to mind.)[1]

This means that man falls a prey to an existence which is no true existence, in fact to perdition.

That which is visible and tangible is transitory; and therefore any man who bases his life upon it has fallen under the power of transitoriness and death. The man who bases his life on that which is tangible condemns himself to dependence upon it. This will be understood, if we consider the fact that one who tries to use the tangible as the basis for his own security is thereby driven into conflict with "the other"; he has to assure himself against the possibility of aggression on the part of "the other". From this arise on the one hand jealousy and anger, rivalry and conflict;

[1] *Kerygma und Mythos* I, p. 25 and n. 1 (E. Tr. pp. 18-19).

and on the other treaties and conventions, conventional judgments and every kind of compromise. The product of all this is an atmosphere, which surrounds every man at all times and guides his judgment, to which all the time every man pays homage, and in the perpetual renewal of which each man plays his part. This is the source of man's bondage to the fear, the anxiety (Rom. 8: 15) which weigh so heavily upon him. Every man strives to cling on to his own existence and to his possessions, all the time with the secret feeling that everything, even his own life, is slipping away from him.[1]

In contrast with this shadowy and troubled existence, existence in faith, the life according to the Spirit, is the true and genuine existence.

In so far as it is life under the power of grace, existence is set free from the fatal necessity of basing itself on the impermanent and the tangible, or rather, it moves eagerly to entrust itself to the invisible, to the unknown, to that which is not under man's control. This unknown, however, reveals itself as divine love, and encounters man as a future which is not death but life. And inasmuch as grace is also the forgiveness of sins, it sets man free from that past in which he was imprisoned:

The attitude of the man who seeks after security, who grasps at the tangible and clings to that which is passing away, to that which indeed at every moment has already passed away—that is in the strict sense of the term sin, since it involves man's closing himself against the invisible, against God's future which is offered to him as a gift. The man who opens his heart to grace receives the forgiveness of sins, that is, he is set free from the past. This is also the meaning of the word "faith"—to open oneself freely to the future. Such faith is also obedience, since it involves man's turning away from himself, his surrender of all security, his abandonment of the effort to gain significance, to gain his own life, the renunciation of all self-confidence, and the resolution to trust only in God who calls the dead to life (2 Cor. 1: 9), who calls that which is not into being (Rom. 4: 17); it involves a total self-surrender to God, which expects everything from God and nothing from itself; and, consequent on this, deliverance from everything tangible and worldly, an attitude of detachment from the world, and so of freedom.[2]

[1] *Kerygma und Mythos* I, p. 30 (E. Tr. pp. 18-19).   [2] *ibid.*, p. 29 (E. Tr. pp. 19-20).

This detachment from the world is, as we have seen, not to be taken in an ascetic sense, but finds expression in the Pauline formula "to possess as though not possessing" (1 Cor. 7: 29-31). It is, then, a form of mastery over the world that is passing away, which can express itself as serene acceptance, in rejoicing with those that do rejoice, and weeping with those that weep (Rom. 12: 15).

This new existence can be defined as "eschatological existence", inasmuch as it is based, far beyond any transitory foundation, on that which is invisible and intangible. It thus makes actual in time, in the present, that existence on the far side of judgment, that existence in grace, which the apocalyptic myth expects to be revealed at the end of the days, and which the Gnostic myth recognizes as an eternal reality (in that sense already present) but confuses with a cosmic process understood in a naturalistic sense. But a process within the merely natural order is not the same as eschatological existence, the life in the spirit. On the contrary, as we have already seen, the indicative which affirms that grace has already come, that the Spirit has been given, that the ἔσχατον, the last event, is already present in time, is constantly transformed into an imperative: "If we live by the Spirit, let us also walk by the Spirit" (Gal. 5: 25).

And when the fruits of the Spirit are enumerated—love, joy, peace, longsuffering, gentleness, goodness, faithfulness, meekness, temperance—it becomes clear that the attitude of faith, just because it involves deliverance from the world, at the same time sets man free for life in fellowship with his fellow-men. Inasmuch as man is set free from anxiety, from his convulsive clinging to the visible and tangible, he is open to fellowship with other men. Faith is defined by Paul as that which "worketh through love" (Gal. 5: 6); it is this attitude which is called the new creation (Gal. 6: 15).[1]

It is hardly necessary to set forth the very close resemblance between this understanding of man, and that proposed in our day by the existentialists.

In particular [to quote a brief summary given by Bultmann himself] Martin Heidegger's existential analysis of the nature of being

[1] *ibid.*, p. 31 (E. Tr. p. 22).

appears to be nothing more than a secularized and philosophical exposition of the New Testament view of man's being; man, who in his historical existence, lives ever in anxiety about himself on the basis of dread, man who lives ever in the moment of decision between the past and the future, whether to lose himself in the impersonal world of the visible and tangible or to gain his own authentic existence by the abandonment of all security and by committing himself without reservation to the future! Is this not exactly the New Testament understanding of man? The objection is sometimes raised that I interpret the New Testament in the categories of Heidegger's existential philosophy. It seems to me that those who so object are blind to the real problem which forces itself upon us. We ought, it seems to me, rather to be disturbed by the fact that philosophy, independently and of itself, has come to affirm that which the New Testament proclaims.[1]

We are concerned here not only with the description of the miserable condition of man in his "actual existence"; the philosophical discovery of the authentic existence of man may bear the closest possible resemblance to that analysis of the structure of faith and of eschatological existence, which Bultmann has worked out from the New Testament. One example of this is to be found in the volume of Wilhelm Kamlah, *Christianity and the Affirmation of the Self*,[2] from which Bultmann quotes. Here the true "historical existence of man" is understood as self-surrender to the totality of being, to the origin of man himself, to God, as the abandonment of all claim to "autonomy" (*Eigenmächtigkeit*); and this is the condition for the discovery of the meaning of man's essential being.

Kamlah himself sees that the structure of this self-surrender is closely akin to the structure of faith, when he affirms that "theologians frequently observe the paradoxical nature of the 'ability to trust' in relation to the first beginnings of faith. The question has constantly been asked how it is possible for the individual to attain to faith, if faith is in fact a gift of the grace of God which cannot be acquired by any independent efforts on the part of man; and how faith can be required of man, if it is beyond the power of man to achieve it. In all too many cases the question has been left unanswered, because the theologians have failed to

---

[1] *Kerygma und Mythos* I, p. 33 (E. Tr. pp. 24-25).
[2] *Christentum und Selbstbehauptung* (Frankfort 1940).

note that this problem is not peculiar to Christianity, but is closely related to a basic structure of our natural being."[1]

We note, then, a close affinity between the existentialist philosophy and the Christian understanding of man, not only in its negative aspect as a description of the unauthentic and ephemeral existence of man in his world, but also in the direction in which it looks for a solution, "salvation", and in its conviction that this solution cannot be anything other than the "true understanding of the self", the discovery of "man's authentic existence". But this raises again, in a new and acute form, the problem which had already been raised by idealism in its classic period, though on a different level, and, it must be added, on a very different scale, though with far less fidelity in essentials to the Christian understanding of man. This is the problem: Can religion be resolved into philosophy? May it not be that idealism (and now existentialism) is the modern form, simplified and completely "demythologized", of Christian faith?

The problem may be formulated as follows: Is it possible to attain to "the true understanding of the self" by means of philosophical meditation and of the withdrawal of man upon himself, by means of pure reflection, although this meditation and this discovery have nothing specifically Christian about them? Is a "natural" faith, a "natural" self-surrender possible? Is it possible without Christ to discover and to share in the genuine existence of man? This problem is made all the more urgent by the fact that, in Bultmann's analysis of the existence of man before the coming of faith and of his existence in the domain of faith, set forth in the few pages of the Essay on the New Testament and Mythology which we have summarized, the name of Christ does not anywhere occur; and if it did occur, we might be inclined to think that it was simply a symbol, a convenient expression for the "existence of the believer", for "eschatological existence". And man, so it seems, can be thought of as possibly attaining to this existence independently of faith in Christ. We must add, as Bultmann does, that even in the New Testament faith is not a sort of superhuman, supernatural quality which has been magically conferred on man;

[1] *Kerygma und Mythos* I, p. 34, quoting Kamlah, *op. cit.*, p. 321 (E. Tr. p. 25).

what it is is an attitude, or rather the true attitude of man; and, if eschatological existence is a "new creation", precisely by the fact that it is "creation" it indicates that man is entering on that existence which it was always intended that he should have. Is it not possible to admit that this might be discovered in some independent way, and furthermore that once discovered it might be followed and professed and lived out without any reference to Christ—unless, let us add, we are willing to use the name "Christ" as no more than a symbol of the fact of this existential discovery?

The problem is not simply historical. Simply as a fact of history, it is plain that that understanding of man which in a thousand visible or invisible ways is intricately interwoven with the whole of modern thought is Christian in its origins. It is impossible to understand idealism (to which reference was made a little earlier) without reference to Christianity; much less is it possible to understand existentialism, the genealogical tree of which is clear and openly admitted: Kierkegaard, Luther, Paul. But the problem of the historical origin of a form of thought is not the same as that of its real basis; and "the fact that the New Testament concept of faith can be expressed in secular terms demonstrates that Christian existence has about it nothing mysterious or supernatural."[1]

The problem is whether man as he is has the capacity to bring his true "nature" into actual existence. Philosophy, in all or almost all its divergent forms, affirms that he can. No other evidence is needed than that attractive maxim of idealism, "Become what you are", *Werde der du bist*. This maxim admits that man has to a certain extent lost his true nature, since it is necessary for him to recover it through becoming. But since the question at issue is that of his true nature, that which intimately and intrinsically he already *is*, no doubt whatever can be entertained as to the possibility of his becoming that which he should be. Existentialism also says to man in another way, "Become that which you are", *Werde der du bist*, inasmuch as it calls man to rise out of the impersonal realm and to lift himself to the level of his own true being. Christianity also says to man, "Become that which you are". But, and herein lies the

---

[1] *Kerygma und Mythos* I, p. 35 (E. Tr. pp. 26-27).

difference, it does not say this to men in general, it says it only
to believers; and makes it plain that what they intrinsically are,
what they are to become, is before all else a gift; that their new
nature, their new being, is a work of grace:

> The New Testament speaks thus only to the believers, to those
> who have allowed the liberating action of God to take place
> within themselves. It does not speak so to men as such. It denies
> that man's life is already in his own possession; it regards his
> situation as one of despair. Why so? Well, just because it knows
> that man can be and can become only that which he already is,
> and because man as such, man before the knowledge of Christ
> and outside of Christ, is not in possession of his own true being;
> he is dwelling not in life but in death.[1]

In the last resort, the difference lies in our judgment as to the
extent to which man has been affected by the fall. Nothing more
clearly reveals the depths of this difference than the contrast,
which is observable between philosophy in almost every epoch
and Christian faith, in the significance attached to the idea of
autonomy, self-assertion (*Eigenmächtigkeit*).[2] From Stoicism
onwards, the idea of the wise man, the goal which he sets
before himself, is self-sufficiency, inner liberty; and this means
not simply independence of the exterior world with its goods
and ills and its conventional rules, but also from himself, from
that body which forms no part of his true being; liberty in the
sense of concentration on that personal spiritual life which is
a man's true being, which is spirit, is reason, reason identical
with that reason which gives to the universe its laws. And
Heidegger himself repeats that acceptance of one's own existence, as it has been "cast into this world", acceptance of death,
is for man the true autonomy.[3] Now it is interesting to note that
Paul appropriates for his own purposes the Stoic idea of
"authority of the self over the self": "All things are lawful for
me, but I will not be brought under the power of any (οὐκ

---

[1] *ibid.*, p. 36 (E. Tr. p. 28).
[2] On the similarities and differences between Stoicism and Christianity as
understood by Bultmann, see the two Essays: *Anknüpfung und Widerspruch* (1946)
(E. Tr. in *Essays*, pp. 133-50) and *Die Bedeutung des Gedankens der Freiheit für die
abendländische Kultur* (1952) (E. Tr. in *Essays*, pp. 305-25) in *Glauben und Verstehen*
II (1952). See also *Das Urchristentum im Rahmen der antiken Religionen* (1949; E. Tr.
Primitive Christianity), chaps. 4 and 5.
[3] Heidegger, *Sein und Zeit*, p. 263.

ἐξουσιασθήσομαι)" (1 Cor. 6: 12); "All things are yours" (1 Cor. 3: 22). But he affirms this only of the believers, and he limits the affirmation with the antithetical declaration: "but ye are Christ's, and Christ is God's". For the apostle Paul, the self-sufficiency of man, man ordinary and un-redeemed, is sin, because this too is "flesh"; it moves, and cannot but move, in the sphere of the flesh and of sin, even though it may be actuated by the laudable intention of over-coming it, of escaping from its influence, as in the case of the man who is active in performing "the works of the law".

The Ambiguity of "Self-sufficiency", Autonomy

In an Essay written in 1940 and republished in the second volume of *Glauben und Verstehen*, Bultmann discusses with originality and erudition the subject, that has been so often debated from the time of the Reformation till the present day, of Paul's attitude to "the law".[1] In the first place he draws a distinction between the ideas of Paul and the current Lutheran interpretation, which has at times been inclined to read its own ideas into Paul's words. According to Paul, faith sets man free from the law, not because the law is an insupportable yoke (the pious Jew felt it to be a help rather than a yoke), nor because it involves a legalistic corruption of true moral principles, nor because it crushes man under the weight of an intolerable sense of sin and failure. It is surprising how little emphasis on morality is to be found in the thought of Paul. He speaks only rarely of μετανοία, repentance, and does not seem to have endured such agonized crises of moral scrupulosity as did Luther. It is hardly necessary to add that Paul makes no dis-tinction between the ritual aspects of the law, which can be rendered obsolete and in fact have been rendered obsolete by the Christian Gospel, and the moral aspects such as the Ten Commandments, which are of permanent value. His criticism is directed against the law as *a way of salvation*.

The idea of "righteousness" in Paul, as in the traditions of Judaism, is not primarily legal or moral; it is religious. It stands for "righteousness in the sight of God", the divine approbation,

---

[1] *Christus das Gesetzes Ende*, in *Glauben und Verstehen* II, pp. 32-58 (E. Tr. in *Essays*, pp. 36-66).

of which the pious Jew desired to assure himself by faithful keeping of the law. Now the apostle does not deny that it is possible to keep the law, or that the law has positive moral value and high human dignity. But, if it is regarded as a way of salvation, the keeping of the law tends to play in with the desire, very natural in man, to secure for himself recognition, to put himself forward, to acquire some merit of his own. These aims are not in themselves blameworthy, but there is nothing specifically moral, still less religious, about them. This attitude gives rise to that "boasting" (καύχημα), so characteristic of respectable people, which Paul charges himself with having fallen into in the legalistic period of his existence, but which he has now completely reversed, being incapable henceforth of boasting of anything other than "God" or "Christ"; or, if he boasts at all about himself, he can boast only of his weaknesses (2 Cor. 11: 16 ff.; 12: 1-10). Luther, attempting to make plain the contrast between "man's own righteousness" and "imputed righteousness", and translating it into terms of Augustine's distinction between the two kinds of love, goes so far as to regard the religious person's effort to work out his own salvation as an expression of that love of self which is hatred against God. Luther's interpretation, says Bultmann, presupposes a maturity of Christian experience which could only be the product of history, and which we must not expect to find in the early days of Christianity. But that Paul did recognize in that self-love, which finds expression in a man's desire to assert himself in the presence of God, a concealed *odium dei*, hatred of God, may be inferred from his view that anxiety is the natural characteristic of the man who is not yet in a state of grace:

This is not difficult to understand, if in fact life before faith in Christ is governed by the need for recognition. For this is always balanced by a hidden anxiety . . . anxiety that I may be lost if I do not firmly maintain my own position; anxiety lest I may be annihilated if I fail to make something of myself. This anxiety, the anxiety under the threat of nothingness, is however as such anxiety in relationship to God, who calls into being that which is not, who demands that man become as nothing before him, or at least become conscious of his own nothingness, and that he be ready to live henceforth by the grace of God and by nothing else. Man's desire to acquire a value of his own, the effort to establish a righteousness of his own, to acquire credit in the sight of God, is then the primal sin. It includes within itself anxiety in the presence of God, hatred of God; it is rebellion against God.[1]

This way of looking at things has deep roots in the primordial religious consciousness of man. The desire to assert oneself over against the divine power is what is meant by *hybris*; it is against this that the divine power reacts, Zeus no less than the jealous God of the Bible. But note the difference between Greece and Israel. Greek wisdom admonishes man through moderation and modesty to avoid provoking the envy of the gods; but the religion of Israel demands of men the exact opposite of *hybris*, the attitude of "trusting only and solely in God".[2]

This analysis serves to elucidate the brief and caustic comments of Bultmann in the Essay on the New Testament and Mythology, where he declares that that "self-assertion", which from the days of the Stoics to those of Heidegger has been regarded as the height of philosophic wisdom, is, when judged by the Christian scale of values, sin and rebellion against God.[3]

It may be remarked that this definition of sin *par excellence* in terms of *Eigenmächtigkeit*, self-assertion, is characteristically Lutheran, in particular of Luther's teaching in his early days; and there is in it a certain element of that mysticism of the infinite which influenced the young Luther. This connection is confirmed by the fact that it is possible to identify these two influences—the first evidently, the second as it were covertly and by suggestion—in the dialectical theology in its first and more controversial form.

Bultmann's purpose, however, in working out this careful analysis is to make it plain that the negative and depreciatory attitude towards "self-assertion", to be found in Pauline doctrine and in Christianity generally, is in its origin not moral but religious in the strictest sense of that term. "Self-assertion", which from the moral standpoint is excellent, or good, or at least not evil (the natural desire to establish one's value in the

---

[1] *Glauben und Verstehen* II, pp. 47-48 (E. Tr. *Essays*, pp. 53-54).
[2] *ibid.*, p. 52 (E. Tr. *Essays*, p. 59).
[3] *Kerygma und Mythos* I, p. 38 (E. Tr. p. 30).

eyes of one's fellow-men is surely innocent and harmless) takes on an undesirable character only in relation to God, only when it makes its way into the relationship between man and God; or, to put it differently, the fact that it comes to be regarded as undesirable reveals that it moves in a dimension which is religious and not simply ethical; it becomes a sign, an outward manifestation, of a religious relationship.

"Self-assertion" can be regarded as sinful only if it is understood in the context of ingratitude. If this unconditional "self-assertion", through which man excludes the possibility of finding his true life in self-surrender, is in fact sin, we must reckon with the alternative possibility that man's existence is to be understood solely as a gift of God. But by laying claim to unconditional "self-assertion", man has himself shut the door against this possibility, since he now regards his existence as a prize which he must strive for, and which he must by his own efforts make his own. The possibility of authentic existence having been excluded, man is inclined to take refuge in a pessimism which regards life as a heavy burden that has been thrust upon him and which he must carry against his will; or in talk about the right to live; or in the demand for a fair share of the good things of life, etc. Man in his unconditional "self-assertion" is blind also to the idea of sin, and by that very fact reveals the full extent of his fallenness. If the word "sin" is used in his hearing, he regards it simply as a piece of mythological language. But this does not, of course, mean that sin is in reality only mythical.

The word "sin" ceases to appear mythological in that moment in which the love of God encounters man as the power which surrounds and supports him, which supports him even in his "self-assertion" and his fallenness, which permits him to be accepted as that which he is not, and in so doing sets him free from himself as he actually is. . . . This is the meaning of that which was wrought in Christ. Where man cannot act, God acts for him, indeed has already acted on his behalf. . . . Eschatological existence has, then, become a possibility for man just through the fact that God has acted and has brought the world as "this world" to an end, that he has made man himself new: "If any man be in Christ he is a new creation. Old things are passed away; behold, they have become new" (2 Cor. 5: 17). . . . What has taken place in Christ is, then, the revelation of the love of God which sets man free from himself in order to be himself, inasmuch as it sets him free to live a life of self-surrender in faith and love. Faith as the freedom of man from himself, as openness to the future, is possible only when faith is faith in the love of God. But faith in the love of God itself is only a form of "self-assertion" so long as God's love is the product of our own wishful thinking, so long as it is only an idea, so long as God has not revealed his own love. Christian faith is faith in Christ, because it is faith in the love of God revealed. Only one who has been loved can love; only one who has been trusted can trust; only one who has experienced self-surrender in another can learn to surrender himself. We are set free to give ourselves to God through the fact that he has given himself for us. "Herein is love, not that we loved God but that he loved us, and gave his Son to be the propitiation for our sins" (1 John 4: 10). "We love, because he first loved us" (1 John 4: 19).[1]

From Existential Analysis to Decision for Existence

With these unmistakably religious declarations Bultmann makes it clear that he has detached himself from that existential philosophy, the special terminology of which he has borrowed —indeed from the whole of modern philosophy, all of which tends towards a denial of the transcendent dimension. We must take note of this detachment, since it throws light on Bultmann's real intention, and hence on the bearing and the limits of his attempt to translate the message of the Gospel into the categories of an existentialist philosophy.

Bultmann has never undertaken the task of reducing the message of the Gospel to a philosophy of existence; primarily because the Gospel is a message, a proclamation, which demands a decision in the field of human existence, and not simply an existential analysis; secondly, because the understanding of existence, the true *Selbstverständnis*, according to the Christian faith, is directly linked to the message and to the decision to accept it. Christian faith and existentialism can, then, use a common terminology; there can be affinities and correspondences between them; but the one cannot be identical with the other. What Bultmann wrote in the earlier part of his Essay on the New Testament and Mythology, before we reach those declarations which form the very heart and kernel

---

[1] *Kerygma und Mythos* I, pp. 38-40 (E. Tr. pp. 31-32).

of it, might perhaps leave room for a certain amount of doubt. He has admitted that the existential analysis recognizes the fallen state of man, that it can even attain independently to an understanding of the nature of that genuine existence, which ought to be man's existence, but which he lacks the power to attain; that it confuses a situation of right (man ought to become aware of his own genuine existence by bringing it to actual effect), and a situation of fact (man, even when theoretically he knows the nature of his own genuine existence, cannot bring it to effect). There is an element of indefiniteness about these affirmations. Perhaps they reflect earlier positions derived from an Augustinian theology rather than rigorous analysis of the position of philosophy on one side and of the Christian faith on the other.

But if entry into genuine existence is conditional on an encounter with God—and by this Bultmann means a real and personal encounter—then a true understanding of existence is dependent on this encounter; and an existential analysis, which concerns itself simply with the being of man as he is, without taking into account the possibility of this encounter, cannot be identical with the Christian understanding of existence. If the Christian understanding is true, then the other must appear hopelessly inadequate. Even that understanding of perdition, of the fallen state, which seems to be so much alive in the various streams of existentialism, must be held to be basically inadequate from the point of view of an understanding of existence which takes as its foundation the encounter of man with God. For, in Christian faith, even perdition is perdition in relation to God, with reference to him, and not simply a recognition of the impermanence and the transitoriness of man.[1] The more exact statements of Bultmann on the ambiguity of the expression "self-assertion" have in fact set our minds working in this direction. Christian faith recognizes the possibility that that very state which from the standpoint of a self-contained analysis of existence is accepted as the height of wisdom and of moral understanding might be from its own

[1] This criticism directed against Bultmann by Friedrich Schumann (*Die Entmythologisierbarkeit des Christusgeschehens* in *Kerygma und Mythos* I, p. 197) has been in the main accepted by Bultmann (*Kerygma und Mythos* II, pp. 192 ff.).

Christian standpoint no more than a gilded variety of perdition.

To sum up, then, the relationships between the theology of Bultmann and existentialism: he makes use of a terminology, which presents itself as apt for the enunciation of Christian convictions either because of its own Christian origins, or because of a provisional affinity between its formulation of problems and that of Christian faith; but he does not accept the existential understanding of existence, which from the first moment onwards clothes itself in a form that is secularized and alien to that presented by Christian faith. Bultmann accepts the existential analysis, to express the matter in the way in which he himself expresses it, he accepts, that is to say, the philosophical method, the underlying concepts of existentialism. He accepts its challenge (which is in origin a Christian challenge, and now restored by existentialism to its place in Christian faith), to repudiate the unauthentic existence of the average man, and to set before oneself the goal of genuine existence. But within this challenge there is implicit a certain definite understanding of existence. For, as a matter of sheer fact, though not necessarily in the intentions of the representatives of the movement, the existentialist analysis does imply and presuppose a certain fixed and defined opinion, a certain decision, as to the nature of existence. Clearly this is the point at which the Christian theologian must decide to follow his own way, a way determined by his own standards of reference. The existentialist analysis can convey to man his duty to "exist", in the sense of enjoying his own genuine existence; but it cannot make up a man's mind for him in advance as to what the nature of that existence is to be. That depends on a decision which a man can take only in his own particular situation, only by himself and for himself.[1]

It must further be made clear that the "choice" implicit in the existentialist analysis must be regarded rather as a theoretical reservation than as a true and personal decision in relation to a man's own existence:

Certainly, pure existentialist analysis implies the judgment that it is possible to make an analysis of man's being without taking

[1] R. Bultmann: *Entmythologisierung und Existenzphilosophie* in *Kerygma und Mythos* II, pp. 192-93 (E. Tr. pp. 193-94).

into account the relationship between God and man. But can we attach any rational meaning to the phrase "an analysis of man's being in relationship to God", if in fact this relationship between God and man exists only in the form of definite and personal encounters of man with God? A pure existentialist analysis cannot really take into consideration the relationship of man with God because it deliberately excludes from consideration those definite, individual contacts in which existence takes on the form of reality from moment to moment. But, even while it does so, it leaves the door wide open for the possibility of such contacts. If the revelation of God can take place only from moment to moment, in the "now" of existence (as "eschatological" event), and if the existential analysis sets man firmly within the limits of that temporality in which he is obliged to live, it does bring to light a characteristic of human existence which faith and faith alone interprets in the sense that man stands in a relationship of dependence upon God. A formal analysis of being does not undermine the interpretation of faith, indeed it rather illuminates it.[1]

In short, the "decision", accepted as a principle by the existentialist analysis, to exclude from its purview man's relatedness to God must be understood in the sense of a guarantee of neutrality, rather than as a convinced declaration of atheism.

It remains, however, the fact that existentialism has no categories in which the encounter of man with God can be expressed. How then are we to express them? Must we perhaps recognize that we have here reached the limits of the elimination of the mythological factor, that the relationship of man with God cannot be expressed otherwise than in the images of mythological language, that, in a word, there is a residuum of the mythological which cannot be eliminated, if we are to stop short of eliminating from the Gospel the reality of the encounter of God with man, which is the essence of the Gospel itself? The problem is one of the utmost consequence, and Bultmann twice formulates it in his Essay,[2] but he leaves it in a certain measure unresolved. The answer depends on the definition which is given of the word "myth"; and, as we shall have occasion to note later, the definition given in Bultmann's

---

[1] *Kerygma and Mythos* II, p. 194 (E. Tr. pp. 195-96).
[2] *Kerygma und Mythos* I, pp. 40 and 48 (E. Tr. 33, 44).

Essay is highly complex and not free from an element of ambiguity.

Is there then left a mythical element? Anyone who holds that any statement about action on the part of God, about his decisive eschatological action, involves mythology, must inevitably hold that there is. But, if so, this is not mythology in the ancient sense of the term, the kind of mythology that disappeared with the collapse of the mythological world-view.[1]

At the end of his Essay on the New Testament and Mythology, Bultmann indicates the lines of a possible solution; but the problem is so important that he has returned to it in a short Essay of more recent date, to which reference must now be made.[2]

Paradox and Miracle

It may perhaps be said that, behind all objections to the attempt to demythologize the New Testament lies hidden the fear that a logical carrying out of the attempt to its conclusion would make it impossible to speak of God's action at all, or would admit the term only as a figurative description of experiences which in reality are purely subjective.[3]

It becomes, therefore, necessary to declare explicitly that

if the term "action of God" is to have any meaning, it must not be understood as a figurative or "symbolic" use of language; it must denote action in the full, real, "objective" sense of the term. If, on the other hand, we affirm that the action of God is not to be understood as a phenomenon of the visible world which can be observed independently of the fact of an encounter between two persons on the level of genuine existence, it is impossible to speak of it at all, without at the same time speaking of me, the man who has experienced the encounter. To speak of the act of God means at the same time to speak of my existence.[4]

Such language as this is neither figurative nor symbolic, but it is certainly the language of analogy:

[1] *Kerygma und Mythos* I, p. 48 (E. Tr. p. 43).
[2] *Die Rede von Handeln Gottes* in *Kerygma und Mythos* II, pp. 196-208. (E. Tr. pp. 196-211).
[3] *Kerygma und Mythos* II, p. 196.
[4] *ibid.*

In point of fact, when we speak in this way, we are picturing to ourselves the action of God on the analogy of human action, and we picture communion between God and man on the analogy of communion between man and man.[1]

Now, in order to give expression to this action, in its character as incursion of the transcendent into the life of man, all religions make use of one specific term—miracle. But what exactly is the meaning of the word "miracle"?[2] In the common use of the term, which is unquestionably mythological, miracle is regarded as a prodigy contrary to the order of nature, which breaks the regularity of the connection between cause and effect, and sets man face to face in the most open and verifiable fashion possible with the disturbing world of supernatural beings or powers. In this sense the concept of miracle is wholly unacceptable to the modern man, who in all his habits of thought and action regards the world as a closed succession of cause and effect in which no interruption is possible. Moreover, this view is not to be attributed exclusively to modern man, nor is it merely the ripe fruit of that scientific consciousness which dawned among the Greeks and has developed among us since the Renaissance. It is the immediate and inevitable presupposition made by every man, in so far as he works in the world, and expects that the world of visible things will respond to his actions in the manner which he has foreseen. So much is this the case that, among primitive people, miracle itself is regarded as a form of causality, different only in kind from that to which we are more ordinarily accustomed.

As is well known, religious and philosophical criticism has long been exercised on the primitive (or mythological) understanding of miracle, and has extracted from it, as its essentially religious content, the pure idea of an action, of an intervention, of God. But rational religion in all its forms tends to identify the action of God with the regular succession of cause and effect, and therefore with the movement of the universe as a whole, which as a whole must be regarded by a religiously-minded

---

[1] *ibid.*

[2] For a critical exposition of the idea of miracle, see the Essay *Zur Frage des Wunders*, to be found in *Glauben und Verstehen* I, pp. 214-28, to which Bultmann expressly refers in the exposition with which we are now dealing.

man with pious veneration and submission as a manifestation of God's ever-present and immanent providence.

Now against this intellectual and intrinsically pantheistic understanding of miracle, the popular and mythical imagination is right in affirming that miracle is something extraordinary, which cannot be reduced to the regular succession of cause and effect in the world understood in a religious sense. If everything is miracle, then nothing is miracle; and if everything is, objectively, metaphysically, the action of God, then God is in fact identical with the world. Moreover, the mythological understanding of miracle raises the question whether the scientific view of the unalterable connection of phenomena one with another is in reality ultimately valid or not. In this sense "mythology" may be the expression of truth in the existential order. The law of causality is produced by extrapolation from the existence of the man who is bound to his past, subject to the forms of this transient and impermanent world; so, in the final analysis, it coincides with sin, with rebellion against God, with the refusal to be open to the future, with atheism. Man can be set free from this unauthentic attitude towards the world not through any theoretical reasoning but only through a religious redemption; he must recognize, he must encounter in his own existence, the action of God.

This existentialist resolution of the idea of miracle avoids the drawbacks attached to both the mythological and the rationalistic understanding of it. In contrast to the mythological understanding, it does not regard a miracle as a "prodigy", open to inspection by sense-perception, verifiable as one event in the series of observable events, one fact among other facts, but exempt from that general law of causality by which other facts are controlled. The miracle, the action of God, is not one fact alongside of other facts; it is recognized by faith as present in the facts themselves, or in some of them, without withdrawing them from the natural causal connection in which they stand. The sick man who thanks God for his recovery does not thank him for having added something to the remedies which brought about that recovery, but thinks of him as having acted by means of them. The existential understanding does not, however, regard the action of God within the normal order of events as an objective datum, always metaphysically present. That is to say, it does not fall into the trap of the pantheistic identification of God with the series of events in its totality. It recognizes that here and there, from time to time, in ways that are always new and unexpected, within the regular framework of events (which it would not for a moment imagine it to be necessary to deny) on the level of the natural order, God has acted, God has touched "me". Therefore the fact that a miracle has happened is not objectively ascertainable; it is visible only to the eyes of faith. All that can actually be seen is the natural happening, within which the action of God has taken place as another and hidden reality.

The most satisfactory term for this hidden association of the action of God with natural events is "paradox":

> While pantheism believes in a direct identity of the natural event with the divine action, faith affirms the paradoxical identity, which can never be the object of anything but faith, and is sometimes contradicted by the visible appearances. In faith, I may regard an event which concerns me as a gift of God or as a judgment of God, though I am in a position to see it equally well in its natural and historical context. In faith, I can regard a thought or a decision of my own as having been directed by God, without for that reason wishing to detach it from the complex of the more immediate motives within the natural order by which I was swayed. Christian faith is not an "understanding of the world", like pantheism. Pantheism starts from the conviction that everything that happens is the work of God, since it assumes that God is wholly immanent in the world. Christian faith believes that God is at work upon me, that he speaks to me from time to time. It believes this, because it knows that it has been addressed by the grace which encounters me in the word of Jesus Christ, by the grace which opens my eyes to see that "God works together for good in all things to them that love him" (Rom. 8: 28).

> But this faith is not a form of knowledge that can be attained and held fast once for all; it is not an "understanding of the world"; it can only be an event that takes place from moment to moment; it can remain living only in so far as the believer asks himself from moment to moment what it is that God wishes to say to him here and now. God in general, God in nature and in history, is as much hidden from his eyes as from anyone else's.

But in so far as, moment by moment, the thing which actually happens is understood in the light of that word of grace which has been directed towards me, faith must and can accept it as an act of God, even when the meaning of it remains enigmatic to faith itself. If pantheism can say in relation to any and every event, quite apart from what that event may mean for me as encounter, "This is a work of God", faith can say only "In this or that other happening God is secretly at work". What it is that he is doing, since this is not directly identical with the event as I can apprehend it, I perhaps do not know now, and perhaps I shall never know. But I am bound to ask what it is that he is saying to me through the event, even if he is saying no more than this, or perhaps he is saying precisely this—that I must be silent and endure.[1]

We must keep these declarations in mind, if we are to estimate fairly the criticism, constantly made by those who do not agree with Bultmann's theology, that he has dissolved Christianity into the pure subjectivity of an existential analysis.

The kind of "palace revolution" which he has carried out, in substituting existential categories for those of Christian faith, is destined, if we accept the point of view of one of the most brilliant of his adversaries, Helmuth Thielicke, inevitably to end by resolving Christianity into a form of philosophy. The defence offered by Bultmann, shot through as it is with profound feeling, cannot, so Thielicke objects, in any way change this situation of fact, and the best evidence for this is to be found in the contradictions and the obscurity of Bultmann's thought. The "understanding of the self" (*Selbstverständnis*), which is the result of faith, cannot be other than the "self-consciousness" (*Selbstbewusstsein*) of Schleiermacher and of idealism, now brought up to date in an existentialist dress; no longer is it the consciousness of the infinity, the eternity, the universality of the spirit that dwells in me; it is the consciousness of *my* real existence, always mine, becoming mine from moment to moment in that decision of mine which is being constantly renewed. The difference is only secondary; each of the two formulations is simply a variant of the principle of Descartes: *Cogito ergo sum.*[2]

---

[1] *Kerygma und Mythos* II, p. 197 (E. Tr. pp. 197-98).
[2] See Helmuth Thielicke, *Die Frage der Entmythologisierung des N.T.* in *Kerygma und Mythos* I, pp. 159 ff. (E. Tr. pp. 138 ff.).

This interpretation, replies Bultmann and with good reason, entirely misunderstands the direction and the intention, in fact the real nature, of his thought. Only when the category of the existential is misunderstood in a psychological sense is it possible to confuse his explicit affirmation of the transcendental with a reduction of the faith to the level of a purely inward experience. But such a reduction is foreign not only to the thought of Bultmann himself, but also to that of the best representatives of the theology of "experience", such as Bultmann's teacher Wilhelm Herrmann, or the New Testament scholar Adolf Schlatter.[1] Neither for Bultmann nor for his teacher (nor, we may add, for Schleiermacher), is the consciousness of faith a purely psychological phenomenon; and its content is certainly not an illusion.

If the being of man in the true sense of the term is to be understood as historical being, which draws the reality of its experience from encounters (*Begegnungen*), it is clear on the one hand that faith which speaks of the act of God which encounters it cannot defend itself against the objection that it is no more than an illusion—for the encounter with God is certainly not objective in the sense of being an event of the natural order; but on the other hand it is equally clear that faith, being a reality of encounter on the level of existence, not only is not under any necessity of refuting this objection, but cannot in fact attempt to do so without misunderstanding its own proper significance.[2]

Moreover, we must not confuse the "existential understanding of man's being" as a theory, as a philosophical analysis, with the "understanding of the self on the level of existence", a constitutive element in which is the fact of real and definite encounter, and which could not be itself, unless the encounter was genuinely real.[3] We must not imagine that Bultmann is developing in abstract terms an "understanding of the self"

[1] *ibid.*, p. 199, n. 1 (E. Tr. p. 200).
[2] *ibid.*, p. 199 (E. Tr. p. 200).
[3] *ibid.*, p. 201. What has been made clear in these explanations is applicable also to Bultmann's reduction of theology to a doctrine of the nature of man. In reply to a criticism made by Karl Barth, Bultmann affirms that this reduction is to be understood only in an existential sense, and not in the psychological sense that is to be found for example in the philosophy of Feuerbach. The actual being (*Dasein*) of man is inseparable from that world into which it has been "thrown". See *Das Problem der Hermeneutik* in *Glauben und Verstehen* II, pp. 233 ff. (E. Tr. in *Essays*, pp. 234-62) and also *Kerygma und Mythos* I, p. 126.

of man in general terms, an understanding which, once worked out, could be expressed in some objective formulation, and in that way even transmitted from one person to another. The Christian "understanding of the self" is so closely linked to the reality of the perfectly definite encounter (as it takes place from moment to moment) between man and the grace of God, that the smallest doubt cast on the objective reality of that encounter would result in its ceasing to be that which it is, and would dissolve it into something of an entirely different character.

As for the fact that faith cannot demonstrate logically that it really is related to its object, that must be regarded as an element of strength rather than of weakness:

> For the affirmation that this can be demonstrated would be tantamount to an affirmation that God can be known and established outside the world of faith; this would bring God down to the level of the tangible world which can be objectively observed.[1]

Neither the appeal to the authority of the Bible, nor that to the reality of the facts of sacred history, can be accepted as equivalent to demonstration; for their value as proof has validity only in so far as they are understood, recognized and accepted through faith, faith which can never lose its character as the supreme risk, the uttermost adventure.

The Act of God in Christ

We must constantly bear in mind these affirmations about the paradoxical character of the divine action, as we try to judge the nature of that "act of God in Christ" which Bultmann regards as constituting the eschatological event in the strict sense of the term, the origin and the canon of our affirmation of faith concerning the action of God in the world.

On February 26, 1951, Rudolf Bultmann was invited to give a lecture at the conference of Swiss liberal theologians held at Aarau.[2] The theme on which he had been asked to

---

[1] *Kerygma und Mythos* II, pp. 199-200 (E. Tr. p. 200).
[2] The lecture has been reprinted in *Glauben und Verstehen* II, pp. 246 ff., under the title *Das Christologische Bekenntnis des Oekumenischen Rates* (E. Tr. in *Essays*, pp. 273-91).

speak was the Christological confession of faith of the World Council of Churches. It is well known that the Churches which have become member Churches of the ecumenical movement accept as a basis the expression of a common faith in Jesus Christ as God and Saviour. Now the expression "Christ as God" is disliked by liberal theologians; they are inclined to criticize the World Council for an excess of orthodoxy which, on their view, is to be attributed to the influence of Anglican and Eastern Orthodox theology in ecumenical circles. The theological champion of "demythologizing", regarded as he is by many as a new and quite outstanding defender of the old liberal position, appeared to be the very man to express with authority the reservations of the liberal group in regard to the ecumenical creed. The reader of the lecture may find it difficult to be sure of the extent to which the liberal theologians were satisfied with what Bultmann had to say; but his remarks are a most valuable supplement to his earlier writings, as giving definition to his own convictions on the subject of Christology.

He first passes rapidly in review the Christological titles used in the New Testament. He points out that the term "God" is applied to Christ only in a few passages of Pauline or deutero-Pauline origin (2 Thess. 1: 12; Titus 2: 13; 2 Peter 1: 1), and that in certain cases the translation is uncertain. Then, having recognized that the Basis may be of value to the ecumenical movement just because of the ambiguity inherent in it, Bultmann states what in his opinion is the fundamental problem:

> The decisive question must be whether, and if so up to what point, these titles are intended . . . to express something concerning the *nature* of Jesus Christ, up to what point, so to say, they describe him as he is in himself, as an object presented for our observation; or whether, and if so up to what point, they speak of his *significance* for men, for faith. Do they speak, as we may formulate it, of his *physis*, his nature, or do they speak of *Christus pro me*, Christ for me? Up to what point is a Christological declaration concerning Jesus Christ at the same time a declaration concerning me? Does he help me because he is the Son of God, or is he the Son of God because he helps me? If the latter, the declaration "We have believed and known that thou art the holy one of God" should

be regarded as a confession based on immediate experience and not taken as a dogmatic proposition.

We are all well aware that in the early Church reflection was concentrated on the *physis*, on the nature, of Jesus Christ; in the light of the traditions of Greek thought it is not difficult to understand why this was so. But if this is held to imply that I can attain to an understanding of his nature without attaining at the same time to an understanding of my own, we shall be obliged to say of that understanding just what James says of the faith of the demons: "The demons also believe and tremble" (Jas. 2: 19). . . . Now I am convinced that it is possible to say that in the New Testament, or at least in the greater part of it, declarations concerning the divinity or deity of Jesus Christ are, simply as a matter of fact, declarations intended to express not his nature but his significance for faith; their purpose is to confess that what he says and what he is do not derive their origin from anything within this world; they are not human thoughts or events of this world; on the contrary in them God speaks to us, works upon us and for us. Christ is the power and the wisdom of God; he has become to us the wisdom of God, righteousness, sanctification and redemption (1 Cor. 1: 30). I would, then, give it as my opinion that in so far as declarations of this kind are adopted in the form of propositions in which Christ is set before us as an *object* for our discernment, they must be subjected to critical evaluation.[1]

Having first made these reservations, Bultmann goes on to observe that in the New Testament there are some passages in which Jesus is spoken of as subordinate to God, as his instrument and servant, but that there are others, especially in the Pauline epistles, in which, though the equation Christ = God is not explicitly set forth, expressions are used of him which are precisely the same as those that are used of God. This is so particularly in the use of the title *Kyrios*, the Lord. Paul, for instance, speaks without any differentiation of "the grace of God" and "the grace of Christ", of "the will of God" and "the will of the Lord", that is, of Christ (cf. Rom. 5: 15 with 2 Cor. 8: 9; Rom. 1: 10 with 1 Cor. 4: 19, etc.). In particular we may note with interest that kind of substitution, through which Christ as the eschatological judge is practically equated with God; as the starting-point of this process, we may note such

---

[1] *Glauben und Verstehen* II, pp. 252-53 (E. Tr. *Essays*, pp. 280-81).

declarations as that of Mark 8: 38: "Whosoever shall be ashamed of me and of my words in this adulterous and sinful generation, the Son of man also shall be ashamed of him, when he cometh in the glory of his Father with the holy angels".

To be answerable to the *word* of Christ as preached by the Church is gradually understood in terms of being answerable to his *person*, and this is then identified with being answerable to God; conversely, the fact of understanding in this way the truth that we have to answer before the eschatological judgment seat of Christ results in the final judgment being regarded as already present in history, strips it of its mythological trappings, and inserts it into that life which is actually being lived by believers at the present time. As we have seen, this understanding of the eschatological judgment as already present in history has been developed to the fullest extent in the Gospel according to St. John. To consider another set of phrases, the sovereignty (or the kingdom) of God ($\beta\alpha\sigma\iota\lambda\epsilon\acute{\iota}\alpha\ \tauο\hat{υ}\ \Theta\epsilonο\hat{υ}$) becomes the kingdom of Christ or his sovereignty ($\beta\alpha\sigma\iota\lambda\epsilon\acute{\iota}\alpha\ \tauο\hat{υ}\ X\rho\iota\sigmaτο\hat{υ}$), and this takes historical shape in the epoch of the Church, in which the power of the word of the risen Christ rings out; thus the mythological concept of an "intervening messianic reign" which is characteristic of late Judaism, is brought within the categories of history—it is the period between the resurrection of Christ and his coming again.

Now what does all this mean? It means that the divinity or deity of Christ is revealed in that event into which we have been brought through the preaching of the Church, which proclaims him as the grace of God made manifest. Conversely, the fact that this preaching is set forth before us as the word that challenges to faith, that calls on us to make responsible answer, and so pronounces the decisive judgment upon us, finds expression in those attributes of dignity that are ascribed to Christ. They assure us that, of a truth, God encounters us in him, and in him alone.[1]

Furthermore, paradoxical in the extreme as it may appear, all this is said of the real man Jesus Christ. The New Testament is opposed to every kind of docetism. This paradox, when expressed in the objectivizing terms of "nature", led in the second and third centuries to the theological paradox of "very

[1] *ibid.*, pp. 256-57 (E. Tr. *Essays*, p. 284).

God and very man", and to the labour of the Christological creeds which were to reach their term in a solution "irreconcilable with our ways of thinking" in the statement of faith of Chalcedon. The old liberal theology disregarded one of the poles of this paradox, the divinity; the basis of the World Council of Churches seems to leap a little too light-heartedly over the other pole of the ellipse. In contrast to both, the paradox is maintained in its entirety, though not in the terms of a theology that thinks in terms of substance, of objects, when it is accepted as a description of that eschatological event which was accomplished in Christ, and in us by means of the preaching of the Church as a continuation of his work.

It is in this sense that we can say that in him God encounters us. The formula "Christ is God" is *false*, if we in any way take the word "God" as applying to some mighty power that can become the object of our observation, whether our understanding of the word be Arian, Nicene, orthodox or liberal. But it is *true*, if "God" is understood as that event in which the action of God is revealed. But my question is this: Would it not be better, by reason of the misunderstandings that can arise, to avoid the use of this form of words, and to be content to say simply that he is the Word of God? Naturally, we do not escape from the false process of objectivization simply by attributing to Jesus decisive importance as a personality, as a character, as a teacher, as a figure in the history of the human spirit. In this way, too, the revelation in action can be misconstrued in terms of something revealed. But the revelation is truly revelation only as continual event, ever contemporary, that is to say where he, with that which he proclaimed and that which he is, encounters me as the action of God upon me or upon us. But the meaning of all this is that we must not attempt to eliminate the offence of the σάρξ γενόμενος, of the Word made flesh, of the σταυρωθείς, the Crucified, who at the same time is κύριος, the Lord. Revelation does not reach us as the communication of an idea of God, or of the idea of divine grace; it touches us in an individual, in a historic figure, and it renews itself from moment to moment in the preaching delivered by other definite historical figures, who ὑπὲρ Χριστοῦ . . . ὡς τοῦ Θεοῦ παρακαλοῦντος, "on behalf of Christ, as though God did beseech us by means of them", proclaim God to me as the God who can moment by moment be realized as my God. The humanity of Christ belongs to his divinity; this is the offence—

that the revelation is there only in the event which actually took place, and that its divine character cannot be logically proved. And if the term *physis*, nature, is unsuitable to the interpretation of what is commonly called his "divinity", it is naturally equally unsuitable to the interpretation of his humanity.[1]

Bultmann constantly speaks of my encounter with God as constituting decision, in the Christian significance of that term, on the plane of actual existence. In the Christological affirmations set forth in this lecture, he makes plain exactly what he means by these terms. Christ is the act of God in the living historic experience of the individual, not only in the sense that the decision and the encounter occur in the line of, and are occasioned by, one particular historical tradition, in which the words and the memory of Jesus Christ are transmitted from century to century, but because in Jesus Christ the Absolute and Wholly Other acquires for our sakes the lineaments of a recognizable human face. That act of divination by which faith discerns in the historical person of Jesus Christ the presence of the divine mercy, and in which the figure of Jesus Christ himself comes to be associated, and without any sense of profanation in a certain measure to be identified, with that divine goodwill which has been perfectly manifested in him, was made possible for the earliest Christian community by its direct relationship to the actual man who had lived as Jesus of Nazareth. For Christians of successive generations, the act of God takes to itself reality in the preaching of the Church, in which Christ lives again as interpreted by faith.

But the fact that this decision takes place in necessary association with a figure who for us cannot be more than an ideal picture drawn by his followers, or a theological symbol, does not in the least evacuate the divine encounter of its reality. In the decision of faith it is not simply an idea of God, it is the living and true God himself who really encounters man, granting to man together with the revelation of God's love a new understanding of himself and a new life. In such an encounter it can truly be said that Christ is transformed, for every generation of believers, into "God for us".

When this discussion with all its varied elements is taken as

---

[1] *Glauben und Verstehen* II, pp. 258-59 (E. Tr. *Essays*, p. 287).

a whole, it is possible to reach a reasonably clear understanding of the position taken up by Bultmann in relation to philosophical existentialism; the decision of faith, the act of God in Christ, clearly fall outside the bounds of the categories of any philosophy, whether regarded simply as a method of philosophical thinking, or as a rational metaphysical system. It is not, however, possible to reach an equally clear understanding of the position that Bultmann takes up in relation to traditional Christian doctrine. It would be possible to define it as a perfectly clear—and negative—relationship, if we were driven to the conclusion that, as understood by Bultmann, the act of God in Christ really involves nothing more than the pure subjectivity of faith, in which the idea of Christ is brought to life again for us. But Bultmann rejects this interpretation of his position. The act of God in Christ is a reality beyond that of subjective experience; it is encounter with the transcendent, it is miracle, and as such can find its expression only in paradox. We have no right to neglect affirmations such as these.

Are we then to understand that the knowledge of a mythological Christ, set before us in the preaching of the Church, can become for us the occasion of a genuine encounter with God? Such an affirmation would not be in itself self-contradictory. The deduction, however, is obvious that, just in so far as the traditional figure of Christ, the Incarnate, the Crucified and the Risen, tends to be dissolved into a myth, it tends also to be robbed of its power to make the encounter of God with man a contemporary reality.

Ought we then, rather, to recognize that what is offered to us by means of the myth is a reality which is itself non-mythological; that the myth clothes—simultaneously veiling and unveiling it—an event which is genuinely historical, but at the same time is more than historical, an event through which in sober reality our time, the time in which men live, has been stamped once for all with the seal of the Transcendent?

We have been brought back to the problem of the nature and value of myth, and to the place which it occupies in the thought of Bultmann.

3

MYTH, RELIGION, PHILOSOPHY

Bultmann's Definitions

THE discussion of Bultmann's proposals for the removal of the mythological element from Christianity has been made difficult, apart from the intrinsic difficulty of the subject, by the complexity of that which is designated by the word "myth". Bultmann is carrying on a controversy on two different fronts. In one direction he is taking up again the arguments directed by the controversialists of the period of the Enlightenment against the understanding of the world which prevailed in antiquity—the geocentric view, the three-storeyed universe, the hosts of angels and demons that inhabit it, the magical notion of "spirit" and of sacraments. In another direction, he is engaged in a problem of exegesis and of the history of religion, —the investigation of the relationship between the message of the Gospel and the eschatological myths of late Judaism and of Gnosticism, the development out of this of a general theory of the relationship between Christianity and mythology, and as a contribution to this enquiry the definition of "myth" in terms directly related to the history of religions:

> Mythology is that form of imagery in which that which is not of this world, that which is divine, is represented as though it were of this world and human; "the beyond" is represented as "the here and now". For example, the transcendence of God is expressed in terms of distance in space. When this kind of imagery is used, worship is readily understood as an action in which, by the use of material means, non-material powers are communicated to man.

He adds an elucidation, which in any case is hardly necessary: "We are not, therefore, speaking of 'myth' in the modern sense, in which it means hardly more than ideology".[1]

Unquestionably this second understanding of the word

[1] *Kerygma und Mythos* I, p. 22, n. 2 (E. Tr. p. 10, n. 2).

"myth" is wider than that in which it means simply "the view of the world prevalent in antiquity"; yet, on the other hand, there are parts of that other definition which are not covered by this one. It will therefore be advisable to discuss them separately.

Myth as Cosmology

Bultmann's polemic against the *"antike Weltbild"*, the world-view of antiquity, is not of recent date. Many years ago he wrote an article for the German encyclopaedia *Die Religion in Geschichte und Gegenwart* on the place of myth in primitive Christianity; here already we find the same criticisms, almost in exactly the same form, as are to be found in the now famous Essay on the New Testament and Mythology.

Clearly this is the least original part of the position maintained by Bultmann; here he is hardly doing more than echo arguments and considerations that underlay the work of the modern school of interpretation of the mythological, and that received their most resounding expression in the *Life of Jesus* of D. F. Strauss.[1] It has been noted that in this respect the position of Bultmann cannot be quite so authoritative, quite so joyfully sure of itself, as was that of his predecessors in the nineteenth century, who really believed in the "scientific understanding" of the world, and felt themselves to be charged with the mission of propagating its truths even in the field of Protestant theology. Bultmann, as a philosopher, is a product of the school of Marburg; he knows that science is essentially a method of study, that every world-view is only relative, and has so to speak value only *de facto* and not *de jure*.[2] We may, then, think that, when Bultmann speaks of the modern man, who turns on the electric light, and listens to the radio, and when he is ill gets better with the help of modern scientific medicine, his touching sympathy is a little conventional. This criticism is self-evident. But we have already noted that, in an area much nearer to the centre of his theological interest, his critical dialogue with the philosophy of Heidegger, Bultmann

[1] Reference may be made specially to the study of Christian Hartlich and Walter Sachs, *Der Ursprung des Mythosbegriffes in der modernen Bibelwissenschaft* (Tübingen, 1952), pp. 121 ff.
[2] This objection is put forward by Karl Barth in *Rudolf Bultmann, ein Versuch ihn zu verstehen* (1952), pp. 41-42.

quite deliberately lays down the limits within which every method of philosophical enquiry must operate, in contrast to Christian faith. All the more may we suppose that he is aware of the limitations of all so-called "world-views", a field in which definitions are much less rigid than in that of philosophy.

We must, moreover, note that not everything in the world-view of antiquity was mythological. What we find there is a view which was in its own way scientific, though its science is out-of-date and no longer acceptable to-day. No doubt the crowd of mysterious inhabitants of the three-storeyed universe recognized by antiquity must be classed as mythological; but that does not mean that that world-view really was mythological and nothing more. When Bultmann goes on to enumerate in a single breath angels and demons, Holy Spirit and incarnation, vicarious expiation and sacramental grace, as aspects of that antique understanding of the world which is now unacceptable to the modern mind, he is including in one sweeping unfavourable judgment a number of objects which are by no means homogeneous. We are entitled to challenge his right to do so.

However, this is a fact: whether mythological or non-mythological, a particular understanding of the world was associated with the Christian faith in its early days, and was associated with it because that understanding presented itself to the believers of those days as both true and self-evident. That was the way they saw the world, that was the atmosphere in which they lived. It is equally a fact that that world-view is to-day an obstacle; an obstacle to faith, which is not insuperable, and often can be overcome, but only with difficulty; its existence must in any case be clearly recognized. For example, it is not easy to preach on the Ascension of Christ without arousing doubts and questionings; and it is not enough to say that these form a part of the inevitable "offence" of the faith, since it is quite clear that for the Christians of early times no such offence existed. The "offence of the cross" in which Paul gloried has nothing whatever to do with the acceptance of a world-view which is out of date and unacceptable to-day.[1]

[1] See on this the wise remarks of Bornkamm in G. Bornkamm and W. Klaas: *Mythos und Evangelium, Zum Programm R. Bultmanns* (1952) p. 12.

The problem, then, is a real one, and we cannot think it unreasonable that we should be asked not to make the task of faith more difficult and troublesome than it already is by burdening it with a dead-weight which is in no way intrinsic to it. It is reasonable to attempt to translate the faith, to present it in the framework—of course a relative and provisional framework—of an understanding of the world which will mean something to the man in the street, who in his high school days was imbued with certain elementary notions of astronomy, chemistry and biology, and who from his own contacts with life and labour has built up a complex of attitudes and reactions, which determine the view he takes of the world in which he has to live.

It is reasonable that this should be asked of us; it is by no means easy to see what we should do about it. World-views are not the expression simply of one method of study, one technique, and of the results that flow from them. Deeper than these, underlying them, are certain presuppositions of a philosophical kind, and these as the expression of a total attitude to life and to the world involve in their turn the acceptance of certain ethical and religious standards, which must be neither ignored nor evaded. The world-view which grew up out of the Renaissance and the period of the Enlightenment in general failed to admit the transcendent dimension. Its cosmology did not admit of any space in which an eternal God could dwell; this fact exercises an influence on thought that goes far beyond the calculations and observations on which it was originally based. On the modern world-view God is everywhere and nowhere. The two expressions may be regarded as synonymous. They do mean, however, that it is by no means easy to reconcile such a world-view with belief in God; it seems almost inseparably connected with a pantheistic or atheistic understanding of things. It is, however, possible to raise the question whether this pantheistic attitude is in reality the corollary of a purely *scientific* interpretation of the world; or whether it is in fact due simply to the fact that modern man in the depths of his being has made a declaration in favour of pantheism and against theism. If such a choice has been made, what we are dealing with is a decision which moves, not in the realm of scientific demonstration, but in that of a certain kind of religious conviction.[1]

It is, then, legitimate to ask whether the Christian message can ever be translated into terms of this "understanding of the world" from which the transcendent has been wholly, or almost wholly, excluded. It is legitimate to ask, as in fact Helmuth Thielicke has asked in his discussion of Bultmann's position, whether the relationship between the ancient outlook on the world and the Christian *Kerygma* is not in fact a great deal closer than is generally admitted, whether this was not in some fashion the predestined channel in which, in the "fulness of time" of the Gospel, that *Kerygma* was bound to run, in order to find immediate and direct expression, in order to win the hearts and minds of men. The three-storeyed universe, with its cosmological hierarchy, is an adequate symbol for a very different hierarchy of existences, that by which faith is called into being. In contrast to the modern understanding of the world, all enclosed within itself and unable to go beyond the idea of immanence, this other is

> open to the transcendent, ready to receive the transcendent, and for that reason particularly well suited to make it clear that God is beyond the world, and that he bursts in upon the world in the historical process of salvation.[2]

We may go so far as to say that the mythological understanding of the world, not because it was mythological in its general character but because it incorporated that particular myth, precisely by reason of that element in it which was historically contingent and liable to become obsolete, was the chosen instrument for the expression of the Gospel. We are not to suppose that for that reason the Gospel is destined to remain for ever bound to what for us cannot be more than an outworn error. The triumphant affirmation of the transcendence of God and of his entrance into history, which found such happy expression in that already existing understanding of the world,

---

[1] "This secularized mythology springs from a revolt; the revolt of the divinities of life (*Vitalgötter*), or to use the terms of idealism, of the wisdom of this world, the σοφία τοῦ κόσμου τούτου." Thielicke in *Kerygma und Mythos* I, p. 180 (E. Tr. pp. 162-64).

[2] *ibid.*, p. 205 (E. Tr. p. 185).

stands firm, even though our contemporary understanding of the world has changed and is infinitely less favourable to that affirmation. But this means simply that our affirmation of the saving transcendence of God, instead of fitting itself harmoniously into the mould of a cosmology which is adequate to it, has to be affirmed in controversy with an understanding of the world based on an entirely different set of presuppositions. It must be presented as a challenge; it must be affirmed as setting a limit to that secularized world-view. Perhaps it may take pleasure in that view's admission of its own relativity, and insist on those gaps which it recognizes in the rigorous continuity of the chain of cause and effect; but it will do well not to make these admissions a ground for boasting, as though they were sufficient of themselves to permit of the surreptitious re-introduction of a cosmology which is favourable to the demands of the faith but is in fact out of date.

In this difficult situation, why should not the Christian faith continue to express itself, for the reasons just indicated, in the symbols of a cosmology which is no longer accepted as literally true? Why should it not speak, as in the past, of the "heaven" and the "earth", with all the religious implications contained in those terms? It must of course be made clear that symbols are symbols. We may here take note of the fact that Karl Barth, without any reference to Bultmann, has made a serious attempt in his *Dogmatik* to bring these symbols back into currency.[1] Barth notes that the contrasted terms "heaven" and "earth" as used in the Bible present an analogy, in cosmological terms, to the relationship between God and man. "Heaven" is of course a part of the created cosmos, but it stands in contrast to the world of our experience, just as the "wholly other" of the divine stands even more radically in contrast to the created universe in its totality. But this contrast between heaven and earth, understood as an analogical expression for the divine transcendence, may usefully serve also as an expression for another great truth of the faith. In creating the world and establishing a relationship with it (the covenant, Christ, salvation), God's action of set purpose took to itself a cosmic dimension; just as it had inserted itself into time, and thereby conferred a new quality

---

[1] *Kirchliche Dogmatik* III, 3, pp. 426 ff.

on time, so it now entered into space, and permeated space with a new significance. When we are speaking in terms of the divine action, such phrases as "where" and "whence", "ascending up to heaven" or "descending upon earth" have a real meaning, even though it is clear that they cannot refer to astronomical space, that space of which our senses give evidence.

If we are speaking strictly in terms of faith, and of what we can require of men that they should believe, it is impossible to go beyond the affirmation that the action of God has taken to itself a cosmic dimension. But it is permissible to go a little further in imagination. This must, of course, be a controlled imagination, an imagination that remains loyal to the demands imposed by faith itself; an imagination that chooses the symbols that it uses from the resources of a theistic and not of a pantheistic understanding of the world. But if we make use of imagination in this way, we shall be driven to recognize that the biblical symbols have lost none of their classic value.

When confronted with the claims of such a Christian imagination, Bultmann seems to have no objections other than those which arise from a constant and serious demand that we should not yield too much to the temptations of the imagination, and that, with a critical spirit that will brook no compromise, we must pose the question of what is, and what is not, *true*, both on the level of philosophy and theology and on that of the interpretation of the New Testament. We must not confuse symbols with ideas; we must not demand of men the acceptance of archaic mythologies as though they were ideas essential to the faith.

During the course of our discussion, attention has shifted from the pictorial content of the ancient world-view (the three-storeyed universe) to the value of modern thought as a method for the pursuit of truth. As a result we are faced, both in the statements of Bultmann[1] and in the explanations offered by his disciples,[2] with problems which are of vastly greater import, though less immediately accessible to intuitive understanding. The basic problem is now revealed to be that of the relationship between *critical* thought and *mythological* thought, and of

---

[1] *Kerygma und Mythos* II, pp. 180 ff.
[2] Hartlich and Sachs in *Kerygma und Mythos* II, pp. 126 ff.

the insuperable difficulty which critical thought, such as that of the modern world, seems to experience in entertaining the very idea of an intervention of the transcendent in history and in the life of men.

But this is no new problem, and it is very much more than the problem of the elimination of the mythological elements in Christianity. As we have already seen, Bultmann himself in trying to find a solution for this problem tends to the idea of paradox and of "miracle", in line with that respectable tradition which the theology of crisis has derived from its origins in the thought of Kierkegaard. Indeed he is even prepared to admit the existence of a "mythological residuum" in his own thought, if that is the only condition on which it will continue to be possible to speak of a genuine encounter between man and God. It seems, then, that there should be no grounds for an irreconcilable opposition between Bultmann and his critics, at least as far as concerns his polemic against the archaic "world-view" in terms of which the Christian faith has come to be proclaimed. In the economy of Bultmann's thinking, this serves as little more than an introduction, intended to direct the attention of the reader to the real problem with which Bultmann is occupied—the translation of the Christian Gospel into terms of an experience on the level of existence.

Myth as the Representation of the Divine in Human Terms

The problem becomes more complex when we approach the actual content of the Christian "myth", or in other words that other definition of myth, which Bultmann claims to have derived from the study of the history of religions. Mythology, according to Bultmann, is that form of representation in which that which is not of this world is set forth in terms of this world, in which the divine is set forth in terms of the human.

This is a broad and generic definition; perhaps too broad and generic. It may be argued that, if this is true, anything whatever that is said about the divine, with the exception of a pure theology of negation, will have to be reduced to the status of mythological language; that it includes within this comprehensive definition of myth every form of expression which represents the divine by way of analogy, parable or symbol.[1] Moreover, a characteristic feature of myth is its ingenuous affirmation of reality; the gods really act in the way that the myth describes, and there is no sense of a distinction between the imaginary tale and the reality which it is intended to signify. The moment the myth is elucidated as symbol, it ceases to be myth in the strict sense of the term; in fact, the mythological element has been eliminated from it exactly in the way that Bultmann requires.[2] Conversely, that affirmation of reality which is peculiar to the myth cannot be dissolved into pure symbol without robbing the myth of that religious content which is peculiarly its own. For an absolutely essential part of this religious faith is the affirmation that God, or the gods, enter into relationship with men, that in some way they involve themselves in the world and in the life of men, that they do carry out real actions within the sphere of this world.[3] To use the phraseology of Bultmann, if myth is really to be myth, it involves the assertion that that which is not of this world really assumes the form of that which is of this world, that the divine really assumes human form, that God in the creation of the universe has really taken to himself a "cosmic dimension". When all is said and done, the basic certainty of the Christian faith is that "the Word was made flesh".

"What is left for the Christian proclamation to proclaim", exclaims Karl Barth, "if it can no longer say that it pleased God to humble himself, to become of this earth earthy, an object of human observation, even, *horribile dictu*, datable in time? For if we take 'God' in the sense in which the New Testament uses the word, the power to do all this and the fact of doing it, so far from being foreign to his nature, are in the highest degree appropriate to that nature". Further, we may go on to turn the definition of myth upside down: "For is it not the case that myth in the true sense of the term has always been, and still is, not the representation of the divine in terms of the human, but in reality simply the representation of general relationships which are immanent in the natural and historical universe under the guise of a narrative of superhuman

[1] See Julius Schniewind: *Antwort an Rudolf Bultmann* in *Kerygma und Mythos* I, p. 79 (E. Tr. pp. 47-48).
[2] See Bultmann in *Kerygma und Mythos* I, pp. 123-24.
[3] See Ernst Lohmeyer in *Kerygma und Mythos* I, pp. 141-42 (E. Tr. pp. 127-28).

99

happenings, of a story of the gods?"[1] Among modern myths, Barth refers to the "myth of the twentieth century", the Marxist myth, the myth of the Christian West.

In brief, if Barth is right, myth should be understood as the representation not of the divine in human form, but of the human in divine form. Now this criticism is an attempt to determine what the myth is really talking about. If we are speaking in terms simply of one particular form of *expression*, it is clearly impossible to decide whether the divine, the supernatural, to which the myth refers is really divine and supernatural, or whether it is simply the result of a split in man's consciousness, and of a projection outwards of something from within man himself. There are myths which are simply a projection of human values, desires or fears; there are others which are not myths in that sense at all, but are the expression in spontaneous narrative form of man's experience of a genuine incursion of the transcendent into human affairs.

Karl Barth's criticism (with which other scholars would agree) is evidently based on a most vigorous rejection of the interpretation of religious phenomena offered by Feuerbach and the psychoanalysts. It would indeed be a cause for surprise if the protagonist of the theology of crisis did not reject all such interpretations! Karl Barth in his younger days directed the whole of his controversial fire towards making plain the absolute distinction between "religion", understood as Feuerbach understood it in the psychological sense of a projection of something outwards from man himself, and that faith in the word of God, which from the standpoint of "religion" is offence, judgment and crisis. If we find ourselves in agreement with Karl Barth, it is clear that myth can belong only to the world of "religion", that is to the pseudo-religion of human desires and values raised to the level of the divine; faith, in contrast to this world of myth, finds its expression in the "word of God", the proclamation of the Incarnation as an event in history. This proclamation constitutes the judgment on all myths, and on all forms of religion, Christianity included, in so far as Christianity is an organ of culture and an institution among the other institutions of civilized existence. Even if this

[1] Karl Barth: *Rudolf Bultmann; ein Versuch ihn zu verstehen*, pp. 32-33.

is true, however, we are not bound to exclude the possibility that the message of the Gospel may make use of mythological elements, as it can of other comparable expressions of a "controlled imagination". But in its essence the proclamation, the *Kerygma*, is not mythological, because it is the proclamation of a divine action which really occurred.

Obviously this criticism lies open to the objection that it has introduced into the debate a presupposition in favour of faith, thus claiming a position of privilege for the Christian myth over against all other myths.[1] To this objection it can be replied that the supposed neutrality of those who offer only a formal definition of myth itself conceals a presupposition, and that this involves bringing Christian faith down to the level of pagan forms of worship, treating the one as commensurable with the other. This is exactly what the New Testament itself refuses to do.

Criticism of the Idea of Myth, based on the Content of Myth

Even if we discount all presuppositions derived from faith, it must still be recognized that insistence on attention being paid to the *content* of myth as well as to its pictorial form has in its favour serious considerations of an historical, philological and exegetical order, as has been shown by G. Stählin in his article on myth in Kittel's *Theological Dictionary of the New Testament*.[2]

In general, so Stählin tells us, classical antiquity as represented in its scholars passed an unfavourable judgment on the value of myth. One exception to this rule is Plato, who regards the myth as an extension of the *logos*, the reasoned argument, and, when he has occasion to deal with questions of theology or of the redemption of man, habitually expresses his thoughts in the form of myths (Eros in the *Symposium*; the other world in the *Gorgias*, the *Meno*, the *Phaedo* and the *Republic*; the world and the soul in the *Republic* and the *Phaedo*; the creation in the *Timaeus*). Thus in Plato myth becomes the vehicle, "the final expression of the greatest pagan theology of the ancient world".

---

[1] Thus Hartlich and Sachs: *Der Ursprung des Mythosbegriffes*, pp. 153 ff.; and Bornkamm: *Mythos und Evangelium*, p. 11.

[2] *Theologisches Wörterbuch des Neuen Testaments* IV (1942), pp. 771-803.

Another exception is Stoicism, which regards myths as the expression of a rudimentary philosophy. Otherwise myth is regarded as standing to *logos*, reasoned thought, in the same relationship as fancy to truth, whether we are thinking of fabulous stories with which historical truth can be contrasted, or of the imaginative expression of philosophical ideas, the counterpart to which is rational thinking defended by argument. Aristotle is quite prepared to admit that myth has the quality of giving pleasure, but not that it has that of giving instruction. The Sophist, in the *Protagoras*, faced with the choice between myth and reasoned argument, chooses the myth, because it is "the more agreeable". In general myth falls under the same unfavourable judgment as is passed by philosophic reason on popular religion and polytheism—polytheism with its all too human and morally dubious gods, whom allegorical interpretation virtuously attempts to make acceptable to the consciousness of a more reflective age. The idea of myth, in the judgment of the representatives of the classical Greek tradition apart from Platonism, was fatally compromised by all the most undesirable characteristics of a polytheism which was already out of date. We shall not be surprised to find, accordingly, that in the world of the Bible the idea of myth either is not present at all, or is always accompanied by a clear judgment of disapproval.

In the Old Testament corpus the word occurs only once, and that in a deuterocanonical work (Ecclus. 20: 19). In another passage, also from a deuterocanonical work (Baruch 3: 23) we find the compound *Mythologos* (perhaps "an interpreter of myths"). However, if the *idea* of myth is absent, the mythological itself is certainly present. The religio-historical school of Gunkel and Gressmann has identified in the Old Testament a considerable number of myths, or mythological elements, which were the common property of the ancient East. "However, even Gunkel recognizes that Israel was not a favourable soil for myths, since these are essentially polytheistic; they set the divine in a relationship to nature which is not that of the Bible, and often represent the deity as doing and suffering things which are unworthy of it".[1] Unquestionably Israel took over a

[1] G. Stählin, in the article referred to above, p. 787.

great deal of mythological material from the nations of the ancient East; but all this material was subjected to a process of very thorough adaptation. One of the deepest and most original characteristics of the religion of the Bible is its attitude to history: God enters into relationship with man in history, in which he himself actively takes a hand; or rather, we should say, it is his taking a hand in it that calls history into being, and makes of the history of Israel "sacred history". In the same way the creation of the world itself is, from the point of view of the Old Testament, an event not in the cosmological but in the historical order. It is the first chapter, the solemn introduction to the history of the covenant of God with men, and with Israel on their behalf. Since this is the biblical standpoint, even the ancient myths which it uses have been profoundly transformed; they have been detached from their dualistic basis; they are no longer the expression of that cyclic return which is the characteristic of all purely natural events, and have been constrained to express a "linear" history, in which everything is new and irrevocable, and in which nothing, literally nothing, happens more than once.

We shall hardly expect to find a more favourable attitude towards myth in the New Testament, in which the faith of the Old Testament has grown to its full stature and which moves in the atmosphere of a lively conflict with the polytheistic and syncretistic outlook of the world in which the early Church had to live. The word "myth" occurs only five times in the New Testament, and only in rather late books, the Pastoral Epistles and the Second Epistle of Peter. It is interesting to observe that the attitude of the New Testament writings towards myth reflects the contemptuously critical judgment of the popular philosophy and the rational literature of the time rather than that of the Platonic tradition. Myth is un- hesitatingly identified with "fable": "Neither to give heed to fables (μῦθοι) and endless genealogies" (1 Tim. 1: 4); "Refuse profane and old wives' fables" (μῦθοι; 1 Tim. 4: 7); "and will turn away their ears from the truth, and turn aside unto fables" (μῦθοι; 2 Tim. 4: 4); "Reprove them sharply, that they may be sound in the faith, not giving heed to Jewish fables (μῦθοι), and commandments of men who turn away from the truth" (ἀλήθεια; Titus 1: 13-14); "We did not follow cunningly devised fables (σεσοφισμένοις μύθοις), when we made known unto you the power and coming of our Lord Jesus Christ, but we were eyewitnesses of his majesty" (ἐπόπται τῆς ἐκείνου μεγαλειότητος; 2 Pet. 1: 16).

It is of no particular importance to identify the myths that were rejected with such disdain; it may be supposed that they were the first speculations of a Judaeo-Christian Gnosticism. It is important, on the other hand, to recognize that the term "myth" is used in an unmistakably pejorative sense; there is no doubt either as to the implications of the word "myth", or as to the emphatic rejection of them. With the myths are contrasted "the words of the faith, and of the good doctrine" (λόγοι τῆς πίστεως καὶ τῆς καλῆς διδασκαλίας; 1 Tim. 4: 6), that is, the proclamation of those historic facts in which the "majesty of God" shone forth, and of which the apostles were the direct and personal eyewitnesses. In the passage of 2 Peter already quoted (1: 19), the phrase used of the proclamation of the Gospel is προφητικὸς λόγος, the prophetic word, clearly in the sense of the proclamation of historic events, verifiable beyond all shadow of doubt, but pregnant with a transcendent meaning; the μεγαλεῖα τοῦ Θεοῦ, those mighty works of God, which, to the utter astonishment of the listeners, Peter had proclaimed on the day of Pentecost (Acts 2: 11). Here once again, as in the critical philosophy of Greece, the contrast is drawn between myths and the truth, ἀλήθεια, as we have already noted in the quotations given above. But we must further observe that in the New Testament, and particularly in the Gospel according to St. John, the term "truth" has acquired a new and pregnant significance; it stands not simply for an abstract truth or for an assured historical fact, but for the Word made flesh, that is for "a divine fact with all the specific weight of historical reality" (Stählin). Without doubt Christianity has taken over mythological elements from its Hellenistic surroundings; but even more decisively than Judaism it has brought them within the world of history, indeed, it has baptized them; the Christian preachers presented themselves not as the followers of "sophisticated myths", but as eyewitnesses of the majestic reality of Christ.

It will be profitable at this point to summarize the conclusions of Stählin's exceedingly important article.

The New Testament shows an unmistakable dislike of myth; and this dislike is in line with those positive and negative elements in the religion of the New Testament, which make it unlike anything else in the religion of its time. It may be possible to recognize certain embryonic mythological elements in the Old Testament records, as also in the New Testament in a considerably modified and adapted form; but myth as such has no place in the world of the Bible, whether as direct communication of religious truth, or as parable, or as symbol.

In the Bible the instrument for the communication of divine truths is the Word of God; the concern of the Bible is with that which God says and that which God does.

In late Hellenistic writings myth is used as a form of parabolic expression. But in the New Testament parable is clearly and admittedly a separate *genre*; it has nothing whatever to do with myth; it is a pictorial representation through which the transcendent can be apprehended, and is never imagined to be anything else.

In Hellenism myth has become symbol; but in the New Testament the one central symbol for which nothing else can be substituted is the cross; and "what the cross shows forth in physical and visible form is a harsh and very far from romantic truth of history". No myth is connected with the symbol of the cross; if it were, "the word of the cross" would be evacuated of its meaning (1 Cor. 1: 17-18). The cross cannot be separated from its historical locus: Christ, Calvary. For this reason the term "the Christ-myth" which has come into common usage as a result of its use by the school of form-criticism ought to be unconditionally rejected.

All this is clear and sharp enough. We turn now to summarize the concluding paragraphs of the article, since they open out before us certain vistas of thought, which are valuable in themselves, and to which we shall have occasion later to return:

Myth, we are told, may be regarded as a form of expression for events which have taken place beyond the limits of terrestrial history. But that would involve a complete inversion of the traditional meaning, of all linguistic usage, and of all the associations ordinarily connected with the term "myth". The reality of "sacred" history is proclaimed in the σάρξ ἐγένετο, in "the Word was made flesh", that is, in a historic fact, which is the point of meeting between the history of God and the history of the world. Nothing is to be gained by using of this unique event the general and relativizing term "myth".

It is possible to regard Christ as the One in whom all the aspirations expressed in the myths of the ancient world became history. As Adolf Harnack has put it: "In Christ the primeval figure (*Urbild*) of all the myths has become history".[1] This concept implies a particular understanding of the history of religions. Without expounding this in detail, we may go so far as to say that even in the form of myth are hidden σπέρματα τοῦ Λόγου, seeds of the Word.

We must recognize the importance of these clear statements, commended as they are both by the admirable and copious store of learned references by which they are accompanied, and by the seriously scientific character of the work in which they have been set forth. In the field of New Testament exegesis the *Theological Dictionary* of Kittel is undoubtedly the most important enterprise undertaken in our generation; and the way in which Stählin has handled the problem is exactly in line with the general tone and emphasis of the whole work; for the aim of the *Dictionary* is, by means of careful philological study and comparison, to make clear and to stress the originality of the categories of New Testament thought, in contrast to Hellenism, to contemporary Judaism, and to the classical traditions of Hebrew thought. We can accept without hesitation the affirmation that the idea of myth is not native to the Bible or to the New Testament; and that those who are attempting, perhaps without due caution, to acclimatize it on the soil of Christian faith are undertaking an enterprise which is audacious and at the least paradoxical.

That of which the New Testament writers speak is generically unique, and different from anything that is to be found in the rival religions. The dramas of salvation, which are set forth in

[1] Harnack: *Die Entstehung der christlichen Theologie und des kirchlichen Dogmas* (1927), p. 16.

these religions, take place in the unreal world of a divine adventure, in an eternity without time, which is yet not exempt from that cyclic repetition that is characteristic of all natural events. But what the apostles proclaim is an historical event charged with a transcendent significance. For such a proclamation of such a theme the word "myth" is quite inadequate. Myth, however it is interpreted, is and cannot be anything but the product of the religious imagination, drawing forth pictures and images from within itself. But the gift which discovers saving significance in an historic fact is that of prophetic divination. For this reason Cullmann is right when he suggests that that kind of interpretation in depth of the event of Christ, which contains in embryo the whole of the Christian understanding of history, should be called not "myth" but "prophecy".[1] The whole discussion of the elimination of the mythological from the New Testament has been all too strongly influenced by the phraseology and the way of formulating problems characteristic of the religio-historical school to which Bultmann originally belonged, though to a considerable extent he has later reacted against its ideas and principles.

But even when we have accepted these clear statements and made all the necessary reservations, we are still faced by the undeniable fact that the writers of the New Testament, in order to make clear, both to themselves and to that environment in which their witness had to be borne, their prophetic interpretation of the event of Christ, did have recourse to mythological forms of expression which were widely current in that environment and were intelligible to all. These mythological elements in the presentation are by no means secondary; they reach to the vital centre of everything—the figure of the Saviour, in the various interpretations of him as the Messiah reigning in the name of God, as the eschatological Son of man, as the Lord of the mystery religions. The mythological character of these forms of presentation is evident; their very variety invites us to look beyond them; the New Testament itself invites us to look beneath the husk of these pictorial forms for a deeper truth, the Word made flesh. But even the profound philosophical formulation of the Prologue to the Fourth Gospel

[1] Oscar Cullmann: *Christus und die Zeit* (1946), p. 84 (E. Tr. 1950, pp. 96-97).

is, if we are to believe Bultmann, to be read against the background of the Gnostic myth; even this passage, in spite of its apparent limpidity, stands in need of interpretation. It is precisely this problem of interpretation to which Bultmann has once again challenged us through the arguments set forth (in an excessively negative way, and an unpleasantly provocative spirit) in the Essay on the Elimination of the Mythological from the New Testament.

Myth as Intuition of the Transcendent

It is perhaps because of this feeling that the problem is one which cannot in any circumstances be evaded that few of Bultmann's critics have adopted so decisively negative an attitude towards his position as that which has been outlined in the preceding paragraphs. The majority of these critics take refuge in that other idea of myth which we have seen to be derived from the Platonic tradition; it is true, they maintain, that myths are found in the New Testament; but myth is the natural form for the expression of religious experience, and perhaps no substitute can be found for it. It is only through myth, we are told, that it is possible to describe that paradoxical event, which cannot in any way be reduced to the categories either of rational or of historical thought—the incursion of the transcendent, of "the Word made flesh", into our history.

This position received a kind of official sanction in the first ecclesiastical document that emerged from those discussions of Bultmann's position that were carried on during the war in the circles of the Confessing Church in Germany. We refer to the report drawn up on behalf of the Confessing Church of Electoral Hesse by Hermann Sauter. This was circulated in mimeographed form, and was published only ten years later in the second volume of the composite work *Kerygma und Mythos*.[1]

The starting-point of the enquiry is the tension between mythological thinking and scientific thinking. Bultmann holds the opinion that this tension ought to be eliminated. Is it not possible that a sense of development in the history of the human spirit has

[1] Hermann Sauter in *Kerygma und Mythos* II, pp. 41-65.

tended to make this tension no longer intolerable, through the recognition that these two forms of thinking stand in a relationship of reciprocal dependence upon one another? Naturally, mythological thinking must then be recognized to be no more than one possible form of thought; but it might be the only form of thought in which that which is beyond sense could be uttered and in which the inner reality of things could come to expression, rather in the same way as space and time are generally recognized to be the intuitive forms by which our sense perception is conditioned. . . .

Certainly myth would need interpretation; but the purpose of such interpretation would be to make the tension endurable and not to eliminate it altogether. Interpretation does not mean that we are obliged to find a form of expression other than the mythological for religious truth. . . . but it ought to show why that with which the mythological thought-form concerns itself cannot find expression in any other form; that though the inmost reality remains inaccessible to us, it does yet encounter us and in this way reveals its reality to us; and that faith, even though it finds expression in myth, is as little "self-creating" as "pure" reason, which in fact is "formed" and not simply "formative", receives, but does not itself produce (we recognize the criticism of Kant made by Schlatter). For myth always contains and discloses some piece of genuine insight, which must be preserved (even though at times it may seem to contradict results arrived at by the scientific way of thinking), if faith is not to be changed into a pure abstraction. But this does not mean that the critical interpretation of myth has to be abandoned. Such interpretation holds the balance for the believing acceptance of the myth, so that the myth is to be retained, never for the sake of some secret knowledge, but for the sake of man's encounter with God.[1]

"Mythological thinking has a dimension of depth to which scientific thinking cannot attain, because it seeks the inner meaning of things and of happenings." As Alfred Jeremias put it in relation to the Old Testament,

the prophetic and apocalyptic style of the biblical narratives is completely mythological. . . . The biblical writers make use of myth for the purposes of their writing of history. Myth, in the strict sense of the term . . . is a spiritual creation of the highest order. It is the narration of a heavenly process, which evolves in a

[1] *Kerygma und Mythos* II, pp. 42-43.

logically determined series of motifs, and is reflected as in an image in the event which actually takes place.[1]

Helmuth Thielicke takes up these expressions, and, accepting the Kantian parallel to which reference has already been made in the judgment of the Confessing Church, comments as follows:

[In this quotation from Jeremias] allusion is made explicitly to a heavenly process, which is the real foundation for the mythological representation. This, if we may so express ourselves, affects mythological thinking in the same way as Kant's "thing-in-itself" affects our perceptive faculties, which themselves are conditioned by the Kantian categories. There is then a genuine basis of reality behind the mythological phenomenon. Therefore the myth—if we may put the matter epigrammatically—is not the objective exteriorization of a purely imaginary inner experience; it is the subjective realization (that is, the intellectual appropriation) of a saving event which is itself objective, in fact of that "heavenly process" to which reference was earlier made. The myth, then, uses forms of expression which are subjective and borrowed from human imagination to describe something which wholly transcends human consciousness, and which possesses an objective reality of its own, even independently of the impression which it produced on the disciples and witnesses.[2]

We need not attach too great weight to a comparison introduced by phrases such as "if we may so express ourselves" and "as it were". The understanding of myth, which—whatever value has been placed upon it—has always been regarded as a product of the poetical imagination, in terms of an *a priori* form of our capacity for sensation is so inappropriate that it hardly seems to require lengthy discussion. For all that, two disciples of Bultmann have discussed it with the utmost seriousness. They observe that, even if we grant that the existence of a sensation is an unquestionable empirical datum, the same cannot be said of the perception of a supernatural "thing-in-itself", nor of a form of mythological intuition adapted to the perception of it; and that, even if it were, the supernatural

[1] *Kerygma und Mythos* II, p. 52. The reference is to Alfred Jeremias, *Das alte Testament im Lichte des alten Orients* (4th ed.), p. 5.
[2] Helmuth Thielicke in *Kerygma und Mythos* I, p. 177 (E. Tr. p. 160).

character of that "thing-in-itself" would still await demonstration.[1]

The expressions used by the defenders of the view that
myth has an objective, valid content may be highly theoretical
and hardly defensible; but they spring from the feeling that
we must avoid the complete identification of myth with the
"fables of antiquity", and the resulting conclusion that no
objective truth at all underlies the mythological form of
expression. But on this point there is really no substantial
disagreement. For Bultmann is himself so convinced that the
myths of the Gospel do express certain objective truths that his
whole purpose in re-interpreting these myths is to bring to
light precisely that element of truth which they contain. We
may regard as a definitive expression of his point of view the
declaration with which Hartlich and Sachs conclude their
interesting book on the origins of the idea of myth in contemporary biblical science. Faced by the question whether the
interpretation of biblical expressions under the category of
myth, as a form of expression for that which is universally true,
necessarily involves the dissolution of the truths they express
into truths of reason or ideas apprehensible by reason, they
answer:

> We do not believe that this conclusion is correct. The recognition
> of the mythical character of a biblical narrative does not in fact
> necessarily involve the reduction of its contents, or of the truth
> contained in it, to terms of philosophy. It may well be that,
> granted an adequate method of interpretation, the mythological
> form may be recognized as the husk within which a truth that is
> not the product of human thought is made available to us.[2]

Why then do some critics of Bultmann, in their desire to
restore the credit of myth as a form for the expression of religious truth, turn in the direction of maintaining, as we have
seen, that what underlies the mythological form is a supernatural ontological reality? The answer probably is that they
are afraid that Bultmann's existentialist interpretation may
dissolve the content of the myth into the pure subjectivity of
"the understanding of the self"; they are anxious to safeguard

[1] C. Hartlich and W. Sachs in *Kerygma und Mythos* II, p. 136.
[2] Hartlich-Sachs, *Der Ursprung des Mythosbegriffes*, p. 164.

the objective reality of facts such as the resurrection of Christ, which faith can never consent to surrender, and which are felt to be undermined by Bultmann's critical approach. Perhaps we can go further and recognize in this defensive attitude that spontaneous reaction, which is still so widespread in the Protestantism of our generation, against the "subjectivism" of modern Protestant theology from the time of Schleiermacher onwards; a reaction which is healthy and worthy of all respect, though perhaps at times it is carried too far. But these very hesitations, these reservations, or preferences for statements in terms of objective and ontological reality, present an obstacle to that sympathetic openness of mind towards myth and its function in religion, which would seem to be necessary as a counter-weight to a certain rationalistic coldness in Bultmann's critical approach.

Myth as Religious Symbolism

It is not hard to see that the defence of the value of myth put forth by modern Protestant theology is *historically* connected with the thought of the Romantic period. Any doubts on this subject have been set at rest by the two disciples of Bultmann, whose volume on this subject we quoted a little earlier in this discussion.

The application of the idea of myth to certain parts of the Old Testament, then by degrees to the whole of the Hebrew religious tradition, and finally with considerably greater caution to the New Testament, as carried out between the end of the eighteenth and the middle of the nineteenth century by Christian Gottlob Heyne, Eichhorn, Gabler, G. L. Bauer, was inspired by an interest characteristic of the Enlightenment—to enucleate the truth underlying the fables, to free the reality of the historical facts from the legendary embellishments or the religious interpretations that have been added to them. On these terms, we start by giving the very idea of myth a bad name, and then the task of scientific exegesis is understood quite explicitly in terms of the elimination of it. This judgment is relevant also to D. F. Strauss, who was by far the most important representative of the "mythological school" in the nineteenth century. That there is a connection between the thought of Strauss and the philosophy of Hegel cannot be denied, but the connection must not be imagined to be closer than it really was. It is true that the essence of Christian faith, as Strauss sees it, is remarkably like the Hegelian philosophy. And so without any sense of theological inconsistency Strauss is able to regard the Christian faith as subjectively true, even when engaged in his most destructively critical study of the life of Jesus. But the demands that he is trying to satisfy are those not of speculative philosophy but of empirical historical criticism; he is wrestling with the problem of the truth of the facts, to which Hegelianism, wholly committed as it is to ideal values which can be as well expressed in legend or in myth as in the bare historic facts, is basically much less sensitive than he; the radical hostility of Strauss to myth is closer to the spirit of the Enlightenment than to that of Hegel.

But, alongside the increasingly destructive critical work of the "mythological school", a different and more favourable estimate of myth and of its function in the religious life of humanity was coming into being. Its source and origin—and these names are in themselves highly significant—was in the line of thought which stretches from Herder to Schleiermacher, and finds its fullest and most consistent expression in De Wette. The purpose of the Romantics—let us so style them—was to rescue the bark of Protestant theology from the sandbanks of rationalism and of orthodoxy by emphasizing anew the values of the inner life as understood in mysticism and in pietism, and by interpreting religion in terms of feeling, life, and, in the case of Herder, poetry. De Wette, as is well known, started out from the position of Kant as re-interpreted by Fries, and endeavoured on the basis of the *Critique of Judgment* to find a way to reconcile the scientific understanding of the world with the imperatives and the ideals of the "practical reason"; or, in other words, to reconcile the theoretical reason with moral faith, which as De Wette uses the terms is synonymous with the rational faith of Kant. He finds this reconciliation in a religious judgment which is evidently closely akin to the "aesthetic" judgment of Kant, and to which De Wette himself from time to time applies the epithet "aesthetic". (This use of terms served as the basis for the rather shallow criticism often directed against him, that he stood for religious "aestheticism", a criticism which not infrequently rested on sheer misunderstanding.)

That aesthetic judgment, however, which springs from religious feeling, is the "intimation" (*Ahndung*), the divination of the presence of the eternal in the natural and finite world, and this finds expression in the antithetical and complementary attitudes of enthusiasm, of religious adoration, of resignation or of the sense of guilt. Now such a religious attitude will find it easier to express itself indirectly than directly; if religion desires to express itself, it has no vehicle other than symbol or image; for here the inner significance of faith is a relationship between value and existence, such as cannot be the object either of theoretical knowledge or of ethical faith (which moves in the realm of absolute obligation, and does not pronounce any judgment on actually existing reality). This does not mean—for De Wette any more than for Schleiermacher—that religious feeling is purely subjective, in the sense that the divination, the "intimation" which finds expression in the aesthetic and religious judgment (or feeling), stands in no relationship at all to reality; on the contrary it is believed to apprehend the very deepest truth of reality. But this truth is set forth precisely by means of these subjective movements of enthusiasm, of adoration, of hope, or of the feeling of absolute dependence. It is to feelings such as these, and to that profound reality to which they are related and by which they are set in motion, that the symbolic expressions of religious poetry, of myth, give expression; and for that very reason purely rational considerations can give no answer to the question whether the "intimation" is an intimation of the truth or not.

So, to look at the matter historically, we encounter this attribution of a positive value to myth as the language appropriate to religious faith in a line of thinkers for whom religion is not predominantly or exclusively rational, but is rather a total attitude which in its sharpest and clearest expression is not rational at all, or rational only in a particular way. (After all, the aesthetic-religious judgment also forms part of a rational scheme, and in the broad sense of the term is a form of knowledge.) This way of looking at things could be called irrationalism in religion, if that term was not charged with confusions and simplifications which it is better to avoid.

All this helps us to understand how it comes about that, when orthodox teachers, anxious to maintain the objective reality of those sacred events which Christians are supposed to believe in as things that actually happened, turn their criticisms against Bultmann and try to find a defence for the validity of mythological expression, they leave on our minds an impression of slight embarrassment, and betray here and there traces of presuppositions and requirements derived from a wholly different way of thinking (those, in fact, of the romantic understanding of religion, to which we have just referred); as, for example, when Thielicke, after quoting the Kantian analogy from the judgment of the Confessing Church, goes on to place side by side with it a quotation from Bachofen which really refers to something entirely different:

> Symbol calls out intuition, whereas language (language, that is to say, in the sense in which language abstracts from reality) offers only rational explanation. Symbol directs itself simultaneously to every aspect of the human spirit, whereas speech is constrained to concentrate itself on only one idea at a time. Symbol strikes its roots into the most intimate depths of the soul, whereas speech like a gentle breeze touches only the surface of the understanding. Symbol is directed inwards, language outwards. Symbol alone succeeds in bringing together the most diverse elements into a single unified impression. Language arranges things in order one after the other, and brings piece by piece to the consciousness that which, if it is to be grasped as a single whole, must be presented to the soul so as to be taken in at a single glance. Words reduce the infinite to finitude; symbol carries the spirit beyond the limits of the finite, of the world of becoming, into the realm of the infinite world which truly is.[1]

Splendid! And highly romantic.

Similar remarks, in themselves of considerable interest, can be found in a number of the essays already quoted. For instance, F. K. Schumann remarks that among the Greeks, myth, even in its earliest manifestations, is anything but "primitive"; it is

---

[1] J. J. Bachofen: *Der Mythos vom Orient und Okzident* (1926), quoted by H. Thielicke in *Kerygma und Mythos* I, pp. 176-7 (E. Tr. p. 159).

a form of speech which has a function quite different from that of language in the ordinary sense of the term, language which is adequate in reference to the world of objects. Myth is conscious of its own higher function. It is language of a superior order, in some degree comparable to that of the lyric style which arose out of it; language which is in the highest degree indirect, allusive, extremely flexible when compared with the solid language of ordinary communication, language which so to speak is always transcending itself, which is wholly directed to our capacity *"subaudire"* (to catch that which is unspoken).[1] The Greeks who were present at the performance of the *Eumenides* of Aeschylus were well aware that this was not a play about some old women; but they also knew that the subject of the play was not one that could be expressed in a complex of logical or ontological propositions. Just so, the Christians who read the vision of the rider upon a white horse (Rev. 19: 11) were perfectly aware that the subject of interest was not the colour of a number of horses. "The New Testament is aware of the indirect character of the mythological images; it is also aware that it is itself using them indirectly. But it does make use of them, because no other form of expression is better adapted to that which it has to say." When for example Jesus declares "I say unto you, that in heaven their angels do always behold the face of my Father which is in heaven" (Matt. 18: 10), "it would be impossible to put it otherwise, without its becoming something entirely different from what it is. A removal of mythological elements, which went so far here as to interpret away the 'mythological' concept of angels, so far from elucidating the meaning would simply destroy it".[2]

So also Regin Prenter, after recalling that the centre of interest in the Platonic myths is man and his redemption rather than general ideas about the universe, and that the true purpose of the myth is not to present an understanding of the world but to offer salvation, reminds us that from its earliest origins myth has been closely linked with worship, and that the aim of the cosmological elements in it is not to give answers to the riddles of the world, but to mediate to man the divine

---

[1] See Friedrich K. Schumann in *Kerygma und Mythos* I, p. 200 (E. Tr. p. 189).
[2] *ibid.*, pp. 200-1 (E. Tr. p. 189).

power of which he stands in need. He then goes on to affirm that "it is impossible to avoid using the symbolic language of mythology, since the reality with which it deals cannot be conceived in other than a mythological form". If we succeed in eliminating the mythological elements, all that we shall have achieved will be to transform a living picture of God into an idea of God, or a feeling about him. Then, in place of the mythology which we have driven out, metaphysics slips in by the back door; then, by reaction against scholasticism, Luther's theology with its predilection for the simple pictorial expressions of primitive Christianity most forcefully reintroduces the mythological form of expression into the presentation of the Christian faith. In other situations, if mythology is eliminated, it may be replaced by sentiment or by psychology—a tendency which is constantly present in pietism. But, whether it be metaphysics or whether it be psychology, each transformation involves a subversion of the living picture of God, which can be safeguarded only by deliberately retaining the original mythological form of expression.[1]

W. G. Kümmel also, on the same lines, starts by reaffirming the impossibility of eliminating the mythological element from the message of the New Testament; but would distinguish between mythological elements which are essential and adequate to the message, and others which are secondary and have been interpolated into the message as it were by way of embellishment. The second type can easily be eliminated. Thus, for example, eschatology as the announcement of a judgment to come must be regarded as an essential element in the message. Moreover, it is to be observed that the understanding of the world current in antiquity is here enriched by an original concept of time, which is the expression of a biblical understanding of history, and therefore cannot be regarded as a cosmological element introduced into Christian faith from alien sources. But such details as the description of the Son of man who will come with the armies of heaven to set up his kingdom cannot be regarded as essential. Essential is the resurrection of Christ, which according to every part of the New Testament is "a real divine intervention, which took place

[1] Regin Prenter in *Kerygma und Mythos* II, pp. 81 ff.

in this world at a determinate moment of time"; "this intervention, however, precisely because it cannot be literally described, can be expressed only in the language of mythology". But not all the details in the narrative of the resurrection are of equal importance; and in general, the mythological elements which the New Testament uses as forms of expression must be judged in the light of their relationship to the central message.[1]

Finally, we must not fail to listen to one voice, which possesses particular authority precisely because it does not come from the camp of the theologians or the exegetes. Karl Jaspers, in a critical study of Bultmann which has attracted wide attention, also defends the unchanging value of myths as a "cipher" of the transcendent. Myths may clash and contradict one another, may drive one another out or be substituted for one another; but the only thing that can be substituted for a myth is another myth.[2]

All these observations are certainly highly instructive. They reflect the mature and considered theological position of men who have not failed to profit by the experiences of the Romantic period and of "pure historical science".

And yet it is not unreasonable to ask whether the dependence of this defence of myth upon the familiar positions of the thought of the Romantic period does not to a certain extent diminish its value, by linking it too closely to one particular understanding of the essence of religion and of the Christian faith; whether too much ground has not been yielded to the convictions of the mythological school in taking for granted the presence of myths in the New Testament; and whether this cheerful assumption of a generally favourable attitude towards myth does not rest on a certain ambiguity in the use of the term itself. Bultmann is right when he remarks that, where the mythological is defended in this way, myth has in fact been elucidated into pure symbol, and is thereby robbed of its true character as myth. The transition from myth to symbol is evident in the remarks of Thielicke cited above, and it is implicit in all the others whom we have quoted. But a myth which has been elucidated into a symbol is no longer a

[1] W. G. Kümmel in *Kerygma und Mythos* II, pp. 161 ff.
[2] Karl Jaspers: *Wahrheit und Unheil der Entmythologisierung* in *Schweizerische Theologische Umschau* (1953, nos. 3-4, pp. 74-106); and an answer by Bultmann in *Theologische Zeitschrift* (Basle, March-April 1954, pp. 81-95).

myth in the true sense of the term—it is a myth which has been demythologized. This transformation of myth into something else has in reality already been carried out, implicitly or explicitly, by all those who have undertaken to rehabilitate myth as a necessary form of expression for the faith.

> Without intending to do so, and without reflecting on what we are doing, we frequently demythologize the mythological expressions of the Bible, inasmuch as they have become to us simply symbols which have long since lost for us their original mythological significance. This happens most easily in the poetic writings of the Bible, such as the Psalms, in which the mythological language can often be understood simply as a poetical expression, and may originally have been intended to be no more than this. Every day we make use of images which derive originally from the mythological way of thinking, as when we say for example that our heart is moved to do this or that—a phrase which no one understands in its original mythological signification. But one whose duty it is to interpret the Bible responsibly must be conscious of what he is doing, and must recognize that, in this connection, honesty compels him to be radical.[1]

The Meaning of the "Elimination of the Mythological"

In reality, it is likely that the spontaneous process of the conversion of myths into something else has already been carried out to a greater extent than the religio-historical school of interpretation is generally prepared to admit, not only in the Psalms but in the books of the Bible generally. Such at least is the impression that may be drawn from the long, patient, critical examination to which Bultmann has subjected the writings of the New Testament, not so much in his brief and controversial Essay as in his larger and calmer works, the Commentary on the Gospel according to St. John, and the Theology of the New Testament; and particularly in that lucid synthesis which he put forth in a more recent book under the title Primitive Christianity against the Background of the Ancient Religions (1947).

Stage by stage, with profound erudition and a deep religious sensitiveness, Bultmann shows that the mythological elements to be found in the writings of the New Testament are not, in the last resort, mythological. He shows that they do not intend

[1] R. Bultmann in Kerygma und Mythos II, p. 187.

to be so, at least in the strict sense of the term; they are more than anything else a means of expression, symbols which bear relation to an object which in itself is not mythological, to a profound spiritual experience out of which has arisen a new understanding of life, of man, above all of the self; and which itself, in the faith of those who are sharers in it, is based upon an action of God in their own personal lives, an action connected with a definite act of God in the history of the world. Of this act of God little is actually recorded, and that only with infinite precautions; because the writers are aware that this reality is something that cannot be recorded, and because the main centre of interest of the one who speaks or writes is not in the mere event but in the reality of the experience that he has himself passed through, and of the renewal that it has produced. The myth, in so far as it is myth, gives expression to the other-worldly origin and the transcendent dimension of that reality.

The biblical myths, then, are not myths in the strict sense of the term; they are symbols of something else, and it would be an error on our part to confuse them with myths which are nothing but myths, and so to attribute to the biblical writers an ingenuous naïveté which was never really theirs. In short, it is difficult to avoid the impression that Bultmann demythologizes the writings of the New Testament, not in the sense that he eliminates the myths, but in the sense that he makes plain that these myths are not really myths, and basically never have been myths. But, if this is so, what is there in fact left to de-mythologize? May it not seem that this hullabaloo of academic controversy about the elimination of the mythological from the New Testament has really been a little excessive?

Finally, it is hard to resist the impression that the elimination of the mythological is related not so much to the writings of the New Testament as to the presuppositions and methods of the religio-historical school, to which Bultmann, together with his colleagues in the school of form-criticism, adhered in earlier years. The work in which his whole life has been spent —a work for which we must be profoundly grateful—is just that of passing this method of interpretation through a most exacting sieve, and proving how questionable its application to the New Testament really is. Every time that the historian of religion thinks that he has encountered a myth, more exact consideration compels him to admit that the myth was not really a myth—it was rather the symbol of a faith which in reality is not mythological. Thus it comes about that Bultmann's critical studies, based on the methods of the religio-historical school, arrive at a result not widely different from that reached by Stählin, whose method is to study myths critically, primarily in the light of their content, and the strength of whose contribution lies in his wide application of the criteria of philology and of the history of culture.

The origins of the picture of Christ presented in the Gospels are to be found not in a myth, but in a conviction of faith, which is attempting to translate itself into the form of a theological concept. A theological concept which attempts to find expression in a narrative and imaginative form necessarily takes on the form of myth. It is, therefore, in no way strange that we find in the New Testament pictorial elements of a mythological character. In reality, there are very few. The theological position is developed with great sobriety. In the setting forth of the two chief episodes of the Christological drama, the incarnation and the resurrection, which would have provided materials for mythological description on a large scale, no concessions are made to pious imagination. The basic affirmations of the faith are set forth plainly in the results which follow upon them, in the testimony of the believers, but they are only indicated with reverent reserve in the actual narratives. The parallels in the pagan traditions, with their marriages of the gods and their apotheoses, would have offered an abundance of materials of which the religious imagination could have made use. The New Testament Apocrypha did as a matter of fact make extensive use of them; the *Ascension of Isaiah* and the *Epistle of the Apostles* describe with lavish detail the descent of Christ through the various heavens, in which he assumes the forms of the various ranks of the angelic hierarchy in order to pass through unobserved by the heavenly rulers who are his foes; and the *Gospel of Peter* gives an extensive description (chaps. 35-44) of the resurrection of Christ.[1] Here we

[1] See Martin Dibelius: *Die Formgeschichte des Evangeliums* (2nd ed. 1933), pp. 269-70.

encounter something that could happen, and did actually happen—a double development of the earliest Christian faith; one in the direction of theological meditation, the other in that of mythological imagination. The first line was followed in the canonical Scriptures and in the ancient catholic Church; the second in the Christian Apocrypha and in Gnostic speculation. The most complete expression within the canon of the development of the Christian tradition is the Gospel according to St. John; among all the New Testament writings, this is the one in which the resolution of mythological elements into expressive symbols is most complete and most deliberately carried through.

The discussion of the value of symbols in religion would perhaps carry us outside the range of the discussion of the elimination of the mythological in the strict sense of these terms. This should not, however, lead to insuperable differences of opinion between Bultmann and his critics. When Bultmann's critics affirm the value of symbolic expression in religion, they are expressing a not unjustified reaction against a certain scholastic flavour which is noticeable in his existentialism, and against what Karl Barth has called "the dictatorship of neo-Kantianism in the school of Marburg", in relation to that understanding of the truth to which Bultmann makes appeal.[1] We must accord to religion the fullest liberty, liberty to make its own choices among possible forms of expression for itself and for the transcendent object to which it is directed. Religion is not bound either to accept or to reject world-views; nor is it called upon to take up a position in favour of one theoretical philosophy or another. At this point we may expect to hear an appeal to Luther, to his titanic efforts to rescue the Christian faith from the narrows of scholastic intellectualism; and that is, in fact, exactly what we do hear. But it is also true that the experience of the Romantic period, and also that of the historical study of religions, have made a contribution of undeniable value to this greater liberty of expression.

It remains, however, true that symbols, in so far as they are recognized as symbols, implicitly admit the necessity of interpretation. And they cannot be interpreted by means of other

[1] See *Kirchliche Dogmatik* III, 2, pp. 531 ff.; and also *Kerygma und Mythos* II, p. 108.

symbols—otherwise we become involved in an infinite re-
gression.[1] In this connection Bultmann refers in a note, and
without pausing on the point, to two examples of the interpretation of myth found in the writings of the American
theologian Reinhold Niebuhr, who also upholds the symbolical
character of myth. Thus, for example, the idea of creation of the
world by God means in the last analysis the limit set to the
rationality of the world, and affirms the insufficiency of any
purely natural causality as an explanation of the irrational
element in things. Original sin signifies "a corruption of human
liberty which is inevitable and yet is not natural".[2]

These examples are highly instructive. They show that the
"explanation" of religious symbols does not necessarily lead to
the replacement of an image by a clear concept; but, apparently
in the majority of cases, simply attributes to myth a negative
significance, in that it serves as a limit to logical and rational
concepts. The logical equivalent of symbol is paradox, and
paradox always contains something which is a problem and an
offence to reason. But it is essentially necessary that the problem
should be accurately defined, and the offence clearly identified;
and this the symbol, in so far as it is symbol, does not do; the
"myth" of original sin, a spontaneous pictorial representation
of the human condition, may well serve as the basis for other
interpretations, not all of them necessarily of so "enlightened" a
character as Niebuhr's. The demand, then, that myths and
symbols shall be interpreted, stands; and it has not in fact
been proved that this must necessarily be carried through only
under the forms of rational intellectualism or of scholastic
thinking. Bultmann, in any case, maintains that he is not
exposed to this danger, since the system of ideas into which he
attempts to translate the significance of the Christian faith is
that derived from the philosophy of existence, a system which
basically finds a place for the non-rational:

The anxiety which is felt regarding the elimination of the mythological may in part be derived from the assumption, accepted
without discussion, that there is no possible alternative other than

[1] See Bultmann in *Kerygma und Mythos* II, p. 108.
[2] Quoted in *Kerygma und Mythos* II, p. 187, n. 1, with reference to Reinhold
Niebuhr: *Faith and History* (p. 52 of the German translation *Glaube und Geschichte*,
pp. 46 ff. of the original).

that between mythology and science; and science is understood as that way of thinking which objectivizes existence by equating it with being after the manner of this world of visible things. But is there not another language, different both from that of myth and from that of science? Are we to suppose that propositions such as "I love you" or "I beg your pardon" are expressed in scientific form? And if not, are we to be driven to the conclusion that their form is mythological? There is, then, a language in which existence can find naïve expression; and, correlative to this, there is a science which can speak of existence without reducing it to the status of an object, as though it was a mere thing.[1]

We are, then, brought back yet once again from the general problem of the interpretation of myths and symbols to the problem of that particular interpretation of them which Bultmann offers, that is, to his personal understanding of the Christian faith and of its connection with the existentialist philosophy. It is time to attempt to reach a final estimate of both.

[1] *Kerygma und Mythos* II, p. 187.

Conclusion

CHRIST AND HIS BENEFITS

As far back as the publication of Bultmann's *History of the Synoptic Tradition* (1921), critics objected that in his reconstruction of the early days of Christianity he had accorded far too small a place, indeed hardly any place at all, to the historic Jesus. Bultmann does not go so far as the representatives of the mythological school, from Strauss to Drews and Couchoud; he never questions that, as a fact of mere history, Jesus did really live. On the contrary, he lays the very strongest emphasis on this past historical existence of Jesus and its significance; and he does this, as we have already observed, by appealing in particular to the Gospel of John, the spiritual gospel, stressing the anti-docetic character of this gospel and the importance that is attached in it to the paradox of the Word made flesh. It is necessary to give great weight to this clear and definite affirmation, both for the interpretation of the Fourth Gospel and for any estimate that we may make of the thought of Bultmann.

As Bultmann sees it, the importance of Jesus in history depends for us not so much on his personal existence as on the interpretation of his person that the disciples worked out, when they recognized in his proclamation of the Reign of God the beginning of that Reign, and in his urgent eschatological message the eschatological event which was already present in him, or was about to burst upon the world. Now Bultmann, who is a Christian as well as a critical student of the New Testament writings, is convinced that the estimate which the earliest Christian community formed of Jesus Christ is in all essentials correct, at least in the sense that in Christ the Christian community had really encountered God, and that for it the eschatological event had really taken place.

That community found that in Christ it had received the revelation of a new situation in the sight of God, and had itself been transported to a new plane of existence—the existence which dwells on the borderline of all the transitory realities of this present life, dwells in the presence of God, of his judgment, and of his grace; the existence which the apostle was to describe, of course in mythological language—but of a very transparent mythology—as the existence of "citizens of heaven" sojourning provisionally upon the earth. When, therefore, the earliest Christian community interpreted Christ in the eschatological categories of Judaism, when the Hellenistic Christian community understood him in terms of the Gnostic myth of salvation, the Church was providing a legitimate and authentic interpretation, and one which, by the criterion of intelligibility in the contemporary world of that time, must be judged to have been adequate. What the Church then did has been done through all the succeeding centuries by all those who, in Christ and through that experience of the Church which stands as our example and is permanently recorded in the Holy Scriptures, find themselves once more transported into an eschatological dimension in the very presence of God.

But the net result of this interpretation, which on its positive side is unexceptionable, is that in Bultmann's reconstruction the Jesus of history is resolved, almost without remainder, into the Christ of faith. This is so not only because, according to the standard of judgment which is based on the critical method of the school of form-criticism, the Christ of faith is the only Christ whom we can reach by way of the *Kerygma* of the Gospel; but also because the objective, historical importance of Christ is understood only in terms of that conviction which he was able to inspire. We can, as we have seen, follow the traces of the historical figure through that which remains to us of the teaching of Jesus; in that urgency of appeal, which is common to him and to John the Baptist, but does not in his case as in that of the Baptist lead no further than a moral rigorism of legal cast; which totally transforms the moral imperative by translating it into terms of that radical inwardness which meets us in the Sermon on the Mount; and which —a further great and precious innovation—is associated with a proclamation of grace and of mercy which reverses all narrow-minded reckoning in terms of retribution, and makes of the announcement of the Kingdom nothing less than a proclamation of pure joy. . . . Blessed . . . blessed . . . blessed!

When all is said and done, however, all these motifs are already present in the prophets of Israel—admittedly with less intensity and concentration than here. We seem, then, to be driven to the conclusion that the real historical importance of Jesus consisted less in *what* he was and said and did than in the fact *that* he existed. The *"dass"* (the fact that he existed) prevails over the *"was"* (the nature of what he was), to borrow the language of some of Bultmann's critics. It is no accident that Bultmann prefers the Gospel according to St. John to the other three. This is the gospel in which attention is directed wholly to the one central point—the declaration that Christ is the Revealer, that he is the Word made flesh; but in which the *content* of the revelation, the meaning of the Word, is hardly explained at all, either because it is regarded as being already well known, or because it is treated as having basically less importance than the *fact* that Christ has appeared. He has come to declare the love of God. But in what does the revelation of the love of God consist? In the fact that Christ has come. This, according to Bultmann, is made quite plain in the primitive form of the *Kerygma*, in which only the death of Christ is so essential that without it the Gospel would not be the Gospel; information as to his historical existence comes to be added to the *Kerygma* as a later and subsidiary element, as didactic or edifying material; when all is said and done, the only thing that matters is that he was "crucified under Pontius Pilate".

This almost complete identification of the Jesus of history with the Christ of faith is nothing new; about 1925 it was the common climate of the supporters of the dialectical theology among whom at that time Bultmann was to be numbered. This was a reaction against that simplification of the historic Jesus in terms of his ethical teaching only, which was characteristic of theological liberalism in the first quarter of this century. This liberal interpretation had been rendered untenable, on the plane of New Testament exegesis, by the emergence of Schweitzer's eschatological principle of interpretation, and by the study of the history of religions, which brought back to light those elements in primitive Christianity that make it possible to speak of it as a mystery of salvation. Other members of the "dialectical" fellowship, through reconsideration of the "Christ of faith" on the level of historical and exegetical study, tended to move back towards the "Christ of dogma"; this was in fact the beginning of the recovery of certain convictions which have been held at all times in the history of the Christian tradition, though in the case of these scholars these convictions were arrived at only through a free and balanced re-working of old theological problems.

In Bultmann's case, however, other spiritual needs seem to have held first place in the field. On the one hand, he was naturally more deeply involved than others in the critical problems of New Testament interpretation, which is his own field of special competence; on the other hand, he is more evidently the heir of pietism and of the "theology of experience" of Herrmann, which, revived by his encounter with the existentialist philosophy of Heidegger, has left on his interpretation of the Christ of faith a very deep mark of subjectivism. There is a sentence in the *Loci Theologici* of Melanchthon, which Bultmann quotes very often: *"Hoc est Christum cognoscere, beneficia eius cognoscere, non . . . eius naturas, modos incarnationis contueri"*—"This is what it means to know Christ—to know the benefits that he has obtained for us, and not . . . theoretically to contemplate his natures and the manner of his incarnation." When Melanchthon wrote them, these phrases were clearly intended to contrast the living Christ of faith with the Christ of scholastic theology; Bultmann, by his use of these terms, contrasts the Christ of faith, or rather of Christian experience actually lived out, of "decision on the level of existence", with that Jesus of history, who in Bultmann's critical reconstruction of early Christian history has been reduced almost to the dimension of a pure geometrical point (albeit the central point for the whole of Christian experience).

The result of this re-interpretation is that the position which was traditionally occupied by the figure of Christ in the picture of Christian origins has come to be occupied by the understanding which his disciples had of him, by their faith in him, by their interpretation of him. It is in virtue of all this that Christ is what he is. It was because his disciples, as a result of his preaching, found themselves lifted up to a new level of eschatological existence that he became in fact the eschatological event; it was because the cross resulted in a profound transformation of their "existential" situation that the cross became the saving event; it was because they believed in his resurrection that he is risen indeed. All these expressions are to be found in Bultmann's writings; it is clear that they are intended to have a paradoxical significance, and it would be unwise to take too literally all the element of denial which they might seem to involve. Now the tendency to regard the earliest Christian community as the primary historical datum can well be defended as a prudent method of *historical* enquiry; but perhaps this principle has too readily been transferred to the *theological* evaluation of Christian origins, and of the essential nature of the Christian faith itself. It is hard to resist the impression, in reading the works of Bultmann, that for him the "eschatological event" is not really Christ but the earliest Christian community; or at least Christ in the community, Christ in the living experience of the community. In this sense the objective Christ of history and of dogma does tend to be dissolved into the *Christus pro nobis*, the Christ for us, of the living experience of faith, and his person to amount to nothing more than the benefits that he has procured for us.

We must note, however, that, in contrast to the subjectivism and individualism so familiar and so widely diffused in the pietistic and liberal forms of Protestantism, it is not the figure of the individual believer which comes before our eyes in Bultmann's thought, but that of the community. Bultmann has most deeply pondered the Pauline understanding of the Church; he has spent years in studying the spontaneous, anonymous, popular development of the Christian "message", before it emerges fully into the light of history. The experiencing subject of Christian history which is continuously present to his imagination, both in his investigation of the development of forms and in his researches into the history of religion, is not the individual believer but the harmonious fellowship of the community.

It is hardly necessary to emphasize the importance, from the point of view of spiritual understanding as well as from the point of view of scholarship, of this change in orientation. Under the influence of this interpretation of the origins of Christianity, which is reflected in his estimate of the nature of the Christian faith itself, Bultmann is moving in the same direction as the contemporary Roman Catholic theology of the "mystical body of Christ". Like a large part of liberal Protestant theology, like Schleiermacher and Herrmann, Bultmann tends to reduce Christology to a doctrine of salvation, and the doctrine of salvation to a doctrine of man; he guards himself against the possibility that this reduction might be understood in the negative sense which is to be found for example in the thought of Feuerbach. But the doctrine of man, in which the theology of Bultmann finds its final term, is not a doctrine of the individual man but of the community. To live on the level of eschatological existence is to live in the communion of the Church; and Bultmann interprets the classic Pauline formula "to be in Christ", which has always been the proof-text of individualist mysticism, simply and straightforwardly in the sense of living in the holy community which is the Body of Christ.

Now all this is very live and important, and may contribute a real enrichment to Christian thought, but only on condition that it is understood not as a reduction of Christology to a doctrine of the Church, but in the sense that man's understanding of himself, eschatological existence, the Church itself, are the consequence, the outcome of an understanding of the person of Christ which is well-grounded and confident. The "eschatological existence" of the Church, the benefits of the cross of Christ, the life of Christ in the Church and in the gifts that he has conferred upon it, have always made sense in Christian thought and in Christian piety only on the assumption that behind them lies a real event, an event which—we cannot avoid the term—is objective in the sense that it is not identical with the Church, that it cannot be resolved into the existence of the Church, but is itself the indispensable presupposition for the existence of the Church; and that event is Jesus Christ himself. His cross can be taken up and carried by the disciples, they can fill up that which is lacking of his sufferings, only if the cross was in sober reality the saving event

accomplished by God, only if it really was the judgment—
at the same time stern and merciful—passed by God on a world
which is sinful but is none the less for that the object of his love.
Jesus can live again in the Christian community only if he is
really risen. The existence of the Church can be eschatological
existence, only if the manifestation of Christ was in very truth
the bursting in of the transcendent upon time—in very truth,
and once for all.

There is an expression which is insistently repeated in the
Epistle to the Hebrews, and which has reappeared in the discussions that have arisen concerning Bultmann's statement of
his position: the word "once" (ἅπαξ) "once for all" (ἐφάπαξ).
Christ "entered in once for all into the holy place—he was once
offered to bear the sins of many" (Heb. 9: 12, 28). Such words
declare the unique and incomparable significance of the event
of Christ, precisely as "saving event", *Heilsereignis*—an event
which never can be repeated and never needs to be repeated.
It is no exaggeration to say that the whole of Christian faith
revolves about this "once for all". The whole life of the Church,
the certainty of the believers, the renewal of their inward life,
their joy, their hope—all this rests upon this "once for all".
It is on this basis alone that Christian life becomes a reality—
as eschatological existence, as imitation of Christ, as the fellowship of his sufferings and of his resurrection, as faith, hope, and
love, as the life of the brotherhood.

Now the doubt which has been provoked by Bultmann's
interpretation, and which all his declarations in the contrary
sense have not availed finally to allay, is just this—whether for
him the "once for all" of the saving event has not been almost
entirely transformed into the "moment by moment" (*jeweils*)
of existential meditation, of Christ for us, of Christ in us, and
of our abiding in Christ. The great affirmations of the faith
are in danger of being transformed into a series of "significances", which, just because they are significances and nothing
more, end by being significant of nothing at all. If the "signifies"
of existential interpretation is not related to the "is" of the
saving event, what becomes of the existential interpretation?
If the doctrine of the Church is detached from the preliminary
and basic affirmation of the reality of the transcendent event of

salvation, does it not end by being dissolved into a "man-centred, psychological, or sociological myth"?[1]

Certainly this is not the intention of Bultmann. We must not overlook the repeated affirmations in which he emphasizes the importance of the real humanity of Christ, the fact that man's encounter with God takes place by means of Christ, that he is "the act of God" in time, the "eschatological event" in the true and original sense of that term. The oft-repeated affirmation that a bare fact of the past cannot become the object of faith unless it acquires a cosmic dimension, unless it is translated into a reality in our own personal history in whatever time we may happen to live, must not obscure for us the truth that the "existential decision" takes place not only in a line of historical succession which goes back to Christ but in direct reference to him. Certainly these basic affirmations would have richer and more living content, if the historical figure of Christ as set forth by Bultmann had not—as a result of the critical pre-suppositions which he has adopted—become so pale and evanes-cent; if it had really corresponded to that figure of the Synoptic Gospels, who in Bultmann's interpretation of the gospel plays hardly any part at all, whereas in the reality of the encounter of man with God he plays a part so overwhelming.

It must be added that in the attempt to pass beyond what must be regarded as the limits of Bultmann's interpretation of the Christian faith, we are not in the least helped by the very close and intimate relations into which he has entered with a philosophy which is almost convulsively concentrated on the vicissitudes of the life of the individual at the mercy of the ephemeral and the impermanent; this is not an unfair description of existentialism, particularly in the form in which it is represented by Heidegger in his earlier years. The formula "understanding of the self" (*Selbstverständnis*) may prove attractive from certain points of view; but, in the last analysis, it is too restricted to serve as an adequate basis for the understanding of the content of the message of the Gospel.

There is a real parallel between Bultmann's procedure and Luther's attempt to concentrate the whole message of the

[1] Karl Barth: *Kirchliche Dogmatik* IV, 1, p. 300.

Gospel in the single theme of justification by faith; and Bultmann's appeal to Luther is more than an artificial piece of apologetic propaganda intended to propitiate the theological and ecclesiastical public in Germany. But even justification by faith is, when all is said and done, only one aspect—a very important aspect, of course—of the Christian faith; and perhaps it would not have acquired such a central position as it has in Protestantism, apart from the continuing controversy with Roman Catholicism. The certainty of faith that in Christ the "act of God in the world" was really accomplished has always produced in the minds of the believers other, far wider and more confident echoes, above all the rapt and astonished meditation on the act of God in Christ itself, whether this has found expression in the lyric forms of worship, or whether it launches itself on the road of theological definition. The centre of Christian faith in all the centuries, we may boldly assert, is not "Christ in us", much less "Christ in us" understood within the narrow limits of an "understanding of the self", in which our own person occupies the centre of the stage; the centre of faith has always been Christ himself, or, to put it in other words, *Christ in himself*. The moment the act of God in Christ has been accepted and affirmed by faith, it necessarily takes the very first place in Christian thought and life and worship; and understanding of the significance of Christ leads out into the broad vistas of creation, of redemption, of Christian history, and of a Christian vocation in the world as well for the Church as for the individual. All this may be understood as implicitly contained in the new "understanding of the self"; but certainly it is not readily suggested by Bultmann's use of that term.

But even if we limit ourselves to the Gospel as a message of *salvation*, it cannot be said that the complicated terminology of existentialism is really well fitted to help us to understand it better. We have, indeed, recognized that this criticism is not very relevant to the principal works of Bultmann, his studies in biblical interpretation and in the history of culture; these are expressed in a terminology derived from history rather than from philosophy. In the *Theology of the New Testament*, in the *Commentary on St. John's Gospel*, the particular philosophical angle of the writer suggests points of view that are fruitful and interesting; it sometimes even happens that the phraseology of the Gospel elucidates the existentialist allusions which are brought in with a view to the elucidation of the Gospel! But, if we look for a genuine and regular translation of the *Kerygma* into existentialist terms, we shall find it only in a few Essays, particularly in that on the New Testament and Mythology; and even here we cannot say that this is the most felicitous aspect of these studies. We may be led to think that this is, more than anything else, an apologetic device on the part of Bultmann, and that it is related to his desire to express the Gospel in terms which will be easily intelligible to the men of our day. But we may wonder, if this is the intention, whether the selection of so very esoteric a philosophy as existentialism was in reality a happy choice.

In this connection Karl Barth with his usual verve cries out:

I cannot understand why, in order to understand the Gospel, I must first squeeze myself into this armour. Long live Heidegger —even the early Heidegger, with his narrow understanding of the nature of man! But that his philosophy of that date—as was at one time thought of the philosophy of Aristotle, and as Hegel in his self-complacency thought of his own—should be declared to be *the* philosophy, as though it had fallen down from heaven— that is certainly not the opinion of Heidegger, nor is it the opinion of Bultmann. If it is to be canonized, the only ground on which this can be done is that it is deserving of special veneration as *the* philosophy of *our* time. That does appear to be the opinion of Bultmann. And who would wish to contradict him? Heidegger's philosophy is without doubt one very significant expression of the spirit of the first half of our century. We all think and talk to-day in a somewhat existential fashion. But there are also other expressions of the contemporary spirit. Heidegger himself seems in his latest writings to have passed beyond that phase of his thought which had normative influence on Bultmann; above all, he has passed beyond the narrow limits of his understanding of man.

In America, on the whole, there are as yet no signs of any interest in existentialism; Russia seems to think that she has left it far behind as an extremely bourgeois phenomenon. And I seriously ask myself whether in the rest of the world, even among people of education, there are really so many "modern men" who recognize themselves in its delineation of man, especially in the form which it takes in the thought of Heidegger, that Christian theology should feel obliged—always supposing such obligations ever rest upon it—to accept this special relationship to the existentialist philosophy. . . . What is certain is that, if we take what Bultmann has made of the Gospel in the name of existentialism, though with a certain perhaps laudable inconsistency, we shall find it if not impossible at least extremely difficult to recognize the Gospel in his presentation of it. Certainly, with a little good will and if necessity arises, it is possible to recognize the Gospel even in the hymns and meditations of a Gerhard Tersteegen, or in the dogmatic theology of Biedermann, or even in the Roman Mass. But I do not know for how many men of to-day Bultmann and his disciples with their existentialist interpretation have really made easier an understanding—*re critica bene gesta* a *joyful* understanding—of the Gospel.[1]

But, as we have said, the translation of the Gospel into the form of an existentialist analysis is not really at the heart of the work of Bultmann. What is of fundamental importance in his attitude towards the Christian faith is that which is also the central motif of all existentialism—the demand for a way of thinking that involves commitment, that moves really on the level of existence (*existentiell*, not *existential*). We may regard as a decisive expression of this demand an Essay which was the work of his early maturity (1925), and which has been reprinted as the second essay in the collection *Glauben und Verstehen*, as though to indicate that this really is the starting-point for the whole of his theological work.[2] The title of the Essay is, "What does it mean to speak of God?" Bultmann's answer to his own question is that it is meaningless to speak of God as an "object", since God is "wholly other", and therefore by definition cannot be the object of our observation. To speak of God has meaning, only if we speak from within a personal situation in which God has revealed himself with irresistible urgency as being simultaneously judgment and grace; that means, not to speak about God (*de Deo*), but to speak of oneself as imperatively moved by

---

[1] Karl Barth: *Rudolf Bultmann*, pp. 38, 40. Barth has chosen these three names to exemplify three classic forms of the resolution of the "once for all" of the Gospel into the continuity of a spiritual process—Tersteegen that of mysticism; Biedermann that of the idealist philosophy; the Mass as the sacramental repetition of the sacrifice of Christ.

[2] *Glauben und Verstehen* I (1933): *Welchen Sinn hat es von Gott zu sprechen?* pp. 26-38.

God (*aus Gott*). Objectivizing thought, of which Greek thought is the highest and finest example, is radically unequal to the task of speaking about God; it is really an atheistic form of thought, such as can be the result only of sin.

It is not our business to emphasize the severity of the judgment which Bultmann here pronounces on that Greek world-view (*Weltbild*), which in all essentials is the same as the world-view of modern science. It is more interesting to note that in this earlier phase of his development the contrast which he draws is not that between mythological thought and scientific thought, but between naturalistic thought and thought on the level of existence. Any objectivizing form of expression, any kind of language which translates God into a form of objectivity analogous to the objectivity of *things*, of natural objects, any theology which treats of God as though he were a part of nature, is incurably inadequate to that which it is intended to express; just as inadequate as mythological imagination, and for exactly the same reason; for in the one case, as in the other, what is involved is an objective treatment of that which cannot be treated objectively, the reduction to the natural level of that which can never be anything other than originating cause, as being itself the subject of every subject and of every thought. It is possible to discern, in this profound demand for sincerity and truth, the roots both of Bultmann's existentialism and of his attempt to eliminate the mythological element from the New Testament.

This aspect of the work of Bultmann deserves to be clearly recognized.

It is necessary to affirm, much more strongly than Bultmann finds himself able to do, the truth and objective reality of the historical and supra-historical event which is summed up in the name of Jesus Christ, the Crucified and Risen One; Christian faith stands or falls with the objective truth of these events. But it is also necessary clearly to recognize that Christian faith is far more than the mere repetition of already well-known truths —it is a reliving of the event of Christ in our own personal existence here and now. To believe in Christ crucified means, in quite definite terms, to take up our own cross and to follow him; to believe in the resurrection means to live in the fellowship of him who is both the Living One and the Coming One. To believe in the Kingdom of God means to live on the eschatological level, that is to say, in the dimension of the eternal that stoops down to enter into time. To believe in the Gospel means, in short, to be oneself an incarnation of the Gospel.

Rudolf Bultmann has become, for many people, the symbol of a dangerous theological radicalism. He is himself in part at least to blame for the opinion that his contemporaries have formed of him. His disciples carry forward ruthlessly the work of critical interpretation of the New Testament that he has initiated. Some of his critics urge him to liberate himself from the idea of the *Kerygma*, as from a last residuum of the mythological tradition, and frankly to profess his Christian faith to be nothing more than a philosophy.

But it would be sad if the profound impulse of faith that is the animating power in all the researches carried out by Rudolf Bultmann were to be forgotten or disregarded; if we allowed Bultmann the champion of the "elimination of the mythological" to hide from us Bultmann the apostle of decision on the level of existence, Bultmann the disciple of Kierkegaard and leader in the school of "the theology of crisis".

When this has once again been made clear to the reader, all that needs to be said about Bultmann has been said; and perhaps this is an appropriate point at which to bring this book to an end.

Appendix

BULTMANN AND ROMAN CATHOLIC CRITICISM

R OMAN CATHOLIC theology entered late, and only by fits
and starts, into the discussion provoked by the writings
of Rudolf Bultmann; what set Roman Catholic thinkers
to work was the necessity of producing reviews and notices
of the two volumes of *Kerygma und Mythos*, which were published between 1948 and 1953. The reviews, which appeared in
various specialist periodicals, were in many cases really full-
length critical essays, in which the various aspects of the
problem were set forth and discussed. Towards the end of 1955
these were collected by H. W. Bartsch in Vol. V of *Kerygma und
Mythos*, and together form an extremely interesting statement
of the position of Roman Catholic theology *vis-à-vis* the theology
of Bultmann.

These reviews were followed by a certain number of separate
works: H. Fries: *Barth, Bultmann, und katholische Theologie*
(Stuttgart, 1955?); J. Bernard: *Bibel und Mythos* (Munich,
1954); L. Malevez: *Le message chrétien et le mythe* (Brussels
1954).[1] The remarks that follow are based in the main on the
essays contained in Vol. V of *Kerygma und Mythos* and on the
work of L. Malevez.

The contribution of Roman Catholic theology to the discussion which has so intensively preoccupied Protestant theology
in Germany has been marked in general by calm and objectivity, and by a certain detachment, such as is natural in those
who do not feel themselves directly affected by the problem
under discussion. In fact, in all these writings there is present,
expressly or by implication, the reference back from the
particular case of Bultmann to the general problem of faith and
theology in Protestantism; but mainly by way of a footnote,
and as evidence of a position tacitly adopted by the authors,

---

[1] E. Tr., *The Christian Message and Myth*, London, 1958.

without any sign of an unattractive satisfaction at disagreements manifest in the camp of the adversary. In Germany a perfectly correct attitude has long been the rule in the relationship between the theologians of one confession and those of the other, and in many cases this is coloured by sympathy and cordial friendship; the relationship is one in which the liberty to say exactly what one thinks is the fruit of mutual esteem and serves to increase mutual respect.

But in this case it would be a mistake to interpret the temperateness of the approach as a sign of indifference. If the Roman Catholic critics are in agreement in rejecting the conclusions of Bultmann, they are no less in agreement in recognizing that the demand that the message of the Gospel should be translated into the language and the thought-forms of the man of to-day is not merely justifiable but is in effect inescapable. This is a requirement of a pastoral and missionary nature, imposed upon us by the alienation of our age and of the men of our age from the Christian faith and from the word of God. What we have to do to-day is not unlike that which was undertaken long years ago by scholasticism, *Fides quaerens intellectum*, the faith in search of intellectual understanding (H. Fries in *Kerygma und Mythos* V, p. 31). "This desire to enter into an encounter with our own time must characterize all genuinely theological work, faced as it is with the rather obvious temptations to fall back either into biblicism or into fundamentalism. We cannot be content simply to repeat the message in its biblical form; it must, on the contrary, be translated into terms in which it can be understood by the men of our time" (P. Jérôme Hamer in *Kerygma und Mythos* V, p. 47). In this sense the widespread discussion provoked by Bultmann cannot be without interest for the Roman Catholic theologian (R. Schnackenburg, *ibid.*, p. 100). Naturally agreement does not go beyond this purely formal aspect of the demand. Only Malevez, if I understand the situation rightly, goes so far as to include among those aspects of the theology of Bultmann which can be favourably received "the principle of the existential interpretation of the message" (*Le message chrétien*, p. 117).

Equally general is the recognition of the genuinely theological character of that which Bultmann has tried to do. "Roman Catholic theology will say 'Yes' to Bultmann's affirmation that the New Testament is above all else message, proclamation, *Kerygma*" (Fries, *Kerygma und Mythos* V, p. 38). "What Bultmann offers to us . . . is a theology of revelation" (Malevez, *op. cit.*, p. 115). Whether this theology can be regarded as adequate is another question; but the Roman Catholic critics note with satisfaction that the Marburg theologian has refused to allow his understanding of the Gospel to be reduced to philosophy and nothing else, that he is resolved to hold fast to the "message", and that he has been unwilling to follow the road, suggested to him by some Swiss theologians such as Buri, of freeing himself from the *Kerygma*, which they regard as the final residuum of the mythological element.

This is, in general, the limit of the agreements; then follow the critical disagreements.

Some of these writers believe that what Bultmann has tried to do represents a working out, to its extreme logical conclusions, of Lutheran "subjectivism", which has led by way of Descartes to the positions of existentialism. Bultmann himself has repeatedly declared that what he was trying to achieve was nothing other than a translation, on the level of scientific understanding, of the Lutheran principle *sola fide*; it is natural, therefore, that he should be taken at his word, and that Roman Catholic critics should point to his views as the extreme and logical working out of this principle (A. Kolping, *Kerygma und Mythos* V, p. 23). Professor Karl Adam of Tübingen also stresses this as the source of Bultmann's thought, but not in terms of unqualified disapproval; Bultmann's existential interpretation of the New Testament leads straight back to the Lutheran and Calvinist principles: *sola fide, sola gratia*. It is, therefore, in this sense, authentically Protestant (*gut protestantisch*); and equally in the sense that Bultmann, unlike the liberalism of the nineteenth century, understands the Christian faith not as a natural or immanent religious phenomenon but as an act of salvation accomplished by God in Christ. But his understanding of Christianity itself seems to involve, in a very exact and precise form, the idea of a divinity who is infinitely far removed from the world, and descends upon it vertically from on high in an act of unpredictable predestination (*op. cit.*, p. 105). This is a theology of pure "actualization in the present" (Fries, *op. cit.*, p. 33), which is forced by its own inner logic to take up a position of extreme irrationalism by reason of its rejection of the theological and philosophical principle of the *analogia entis*, the analogy of being (Adam, *op. cit.*, p. 107). Bultmann's thought derives from Lutheran sources, and has an innate affinity with the Lutheran way of thinking. As far as Lutheran theology is concerned, Bultmann is therefore in the strict sense of the term "the invincible"; he is the sign of a profound crisis, for which a solution can be found only through a return of Lutheranism to a theology of the Church, and the recovery of an effective teaching authority in the Church such as can decide and not merely discuss (Adam Fechter in *Kerygma und Mythos* V, pp. 79 ff.).

But these are to some extent marginal considerations, and do not touch the heart of the problem. Most of the Roman Catholic contributions are taken up with a discussion of the problems actually raised by Bultmann, either in the field of exegesis, or in that of the relationship between theology and philosophy.

Of the two groups of problems, it is the second which has chiefly attracted the attention of the Roman Catholic critics— that of the "existential" transcript of the Gospel in close association with the philosophy of Heidegger. The Roman Catholics do not seem to find themselves entirely in agreement with the objections raised by Protestant scholars; indeed they are rather inclined to regard Bultmann's thought as marking a reaction against that exclusive biblicism, that radical distrust of philosophy, which has been dominant in Protestant theology, especially in the school of Karl Barth (Hamer, *op. cit.*, pp. 47- 48). The passionate interest aroused by Bultmann's arguments is held to give evidence of an unappeased sense of need for rationality in the Protestant world, such as cannot be satisfied by the biblical "purism" of the Protestant theologians; whereas the great scholastic tradition, or rather that tradition which goes back to the apologists of the second century and the Alexandrian theologians of the third, gives evidence of a confident association between philosophy and theology, which only Luther was bold enough to break (Fechter in *Kerygma und Mythos* V, p. 77; Malevez, *op. cit.*, p. 41 f.). It is, in a word, interesting to note that the Roman Catholic critics are on the whole inclined to take a favourable view of the demand for a translation of the theological message into the categories of a living philosophy (though the value of that philosophy may itself be open to question); whereas on the contrary "pure" theologians like Karl Barth, and "pure" philosophers like Jaspers, both find fault with Bultmann for what they regard as an undesirable confusion of spheres; to this they attribute a certain hybrid quality in his thought, which in the final analysis does not satisfy either theologians or philosophers.

The strictly exegetical aspect of Bultmann's work is treated as of only secondary interest, but we find that this too gives rise to interesting observations.

R. Schnackenburg of Bamberg relates the question of demythologizing to the presuppositions involved in the method of study adopted by the form-critical school (*Kerygma und Mythos* V, pp. 83 ff.); and in another Essay discusses the Christology of Bultmann, which he contrasts with that of the Council of Chalcedon (*ibid.*, pp. 123 ff.).

René Marlé of Angers discusses the interpretations put forward in Bultmann's *Theology of the New Testament* (*ibid.*, pp. 141 ff.).

Karl Adam, in an Essay already quoted, criticizes the method of the elimination of the mythological in relation to a delicate and central problem—that of the resurrection of Christ. To Roman Catholic theology the resurrection is not simply a material miracle, intrinsically evident to the senses. Jesus revealed himself only to his disciples, and at times it seems to have been difficult even for them to realize who he was. Mary Magdalene mistakes him for the gardener (John 20: 15-16); the disciples at Emmaus recognize him only in the breaking of bread (Luke 24: 31); the Risen One reveals himself only to faith. And that sensible image of the Risen Christ, his actual visible form as a living person, however it may have been brought into being in the minds of the apostles (for, to use the words of Thomas Aquinas: "it was within his power that from the sight of him there should be formed in the eyes of the beholders either a glorious form, or a form lacking in glory, or partly glorious and partly not, or in any other way whatsoever", *Summa Th.* 3: 54 ad 3), did not in itself constitute the content of faith in the resurrection; it was simply the occasion of it, "the cause which brought faith into being from outside". The appearances were simply "the changing reflections of a more penetrating and invisible divine reality, which by means of these visible manifestations entered into the minds of the disciples, took hold upon them, filled them with itself to such an extent that they could not escape from the consciousness of the presence of the risen Christ" (*Kerygma und Mythos* V, p. 117-18).

This experience determined their entire understanding of the earthly life of the Christ, which now expressed itself in the words of Thomas "My Lord, and my God" (John 20: 28). Faith in the Risen Christ sends them back to the Lord himself; this faith, in the strictest sense of the word, is brought into being by Christ himself. Grace, which according to Thomas Aquinas is the true and transcendent cause of faith, finds its fulfilment in the faith of the disciples. And faith in the Risen One is centred in him as the principal object to which it is directed; it is not simply or principally, as Bultmann would have it to be, the certainty of the divine forgiveness which has been granted to "me", the disclosure of the true "understanding of the self", the beginning of "eschatological existence". On the contrary, faith in the Risen One is not concerned particularly "with me", "with us"; it is concerned with the Risen One himself—it is the certainty that in truth and in reality he has triumphed (*Kerygma und Mythos* V, pp. 113-19).

The monograph which L. Malevez, S.J., has produced on the theology of Bultmann contains a delicate and accurate analysis, following closely the most complex nuances of his thought. Malevez rejects as wholly inadequate the "subjectivizing" interpretation of Bultmann's views which has been put forward by most of his critics on the Protestant side, and rightly maintains that Bultmann's real position can be understood only if the "objective" significance of his affirmations, in the theological sense of that term, is recognized. The theology of Bultmann is a "theology of the event", of a real, divine event, which has taken place within the limits of our existence and determines its meaning. Man discovers his own true existence, in so far as he becomes aware that it really is true that God loves him and comes to meet him. This encounter, the objective starting-point of which is the figure of Christ, and the objective continuation of which is to be found in the proclamation of the message of the Gospel, constitutes "the event" in the theological sense of the term, and determines the meaning of the term "history", true history, which as we have seen Bultmann distinguishes from the "mere history" of chronological succession. True history is our own historicity, in so far as that is determined by our encounter with a transcendent factor which is objective, even though it cannot be reduced to the level of such objects as the things that exist in this world. That transcendent factor is the act of God in Christ. The attempt to attribute a false objectivity to this act, to represent it as a reality of the kind that can be immanent in this world of space and time, is that which lies at the root of "myth" properly so called; but recognition of the "mythological" character of these attempts at false objectivization does not involve a denial of the "objective" reality of that act of God which took on personal form in Christ.

These accurate and intelligent observations are all the more worthy of record because we have not always been provided in the Protestant world with so scrupulously correct an interpretation of these fundamental ideas of Bultmann's theology. It is possible to ask, however, whether Malevez' anxious care to emphasize the divine objectivity of the event may not be a little excessive, and whether, in his desire to contrast and to elucidate, he does not make too sharp a distinction between the things that in Bultmann's own thought are not, and perhaps cannot be, so clearly distinguished—the objective and the subjective aspects of the salvation-event.

In recent times Protestant theology has put into currency two terms, which it uses to express its idea of "a history of salvation" (*Heilsgeschichte*), that is, history considered in the light of the dimension of transcendence which encounters it: *Urgeschichte* (primeval history) and *Übergeschichte* (super-history or meta-history). Bultmann, simply as a matter of fact, does not make use of either of these terms. His understanding of "real history" (*Geschichte*) in the Essay on the elimination of the mythological is exactly that of Heidegger; it relates, that is to say, to the historicity of "being in time". Before Bultmann became acquainted with the thought of Heidegger, his understanding of history seems to have been determined by the interpretative principles of Dilthey (see *Das Problem der Hermeneutik* in *Glauben und Verstehen* II, pp. 211 ff., E. Tr. in *Essays* pp. 236-62, and also the Introduction to his *Jesus*); and the movement of his thought from one system of ideas to the other is all the more natural in that Heidegger himself admits that he is indebted to Dilthey for his understanding of history (*Sein und Zeit* §77). This interpretation has been confirmed by Bultmann in his Gifford Lectures on *History and Eschatology* (Edinburgh, 1957).

It seems, then, that Bultmann learned to think in categories derived from history and from culture rather than in those derived directly from theology. It need hardly be said that his own understanding of history is deeply charged with theological significance; but for all that it does not deny its non-theological origin. It has even been maintained that the idea of history in Bultmann is dogged by a certain dualism, in that it contains the lees of a positivist understanding of history, against which the critical work of Dilthey was itself a reaction. In principle, Bultmann the philosopher has abandoned these positivist ideas; nevertheless they reappear in the learned researches of Bultmann the interpreter of the New Testament. The dramatic character which the discussion of the validity of "myth" takes on in Bultmann's theology may perhaps be the result of this residuum of positivist historicism, from which Bultmann has never really been emancipated. (See H. Ott: *Geschichte und Heilsgeschichte in der Theologie Rudolf Bultmanns*, Tübingen 1955, a book which was published after the printing of the present work had been begun.)

These remarks are not intended to detract in any way from the value of the interpretation offered by Malevez, which is in all its main lines the same as our own; but they may serve to indicate the inevitable limitations of such an interpretation.

Bibliographical Note

Rudolf Bultmann was born on August 20, 1884, at Wiefeld-stede in Oldenburg, and the following dates mark the progress of his academic career:

1912. *Privat-dozent* in New Testament Exegesis at Marburg.
1916. Professor (*Extraordinarius*) at Breslau.
1920. Professor (*Ordinarius*) at Giessen.
1921. Professor (*Ordinarius*) at Marburg.

At present he is in retirement. His whole life has been passed in the world of university teaching. During the war he was a supporter of the "Confessing Church".

Principal Works of Bultmann

1. *Der Stil der Paulinischen Predigt und die kynisch-stoische Diatribe* (Doctorate thesis, Göttingen, 1910).
2. *Die Geschichte der synoptischen Tradition* (Göttingen 1921; 2nd ed. 1931: 3rd ed. 1957).
3. *Die Erforschung der synoptischen Evangelien* (Giessen 1925; 2nd ed. 1930).
4. *Jesus* (in the collection *Die Unsterblichen*; Berlin 1926; 2nd ed. 1929. Also in English, Swedish, Danish and Japanese translations).
5. *Glauben und Verstehen*, a collection of Essays, some of which had been published before, others previously unpublished. (Vol. I. Tübingen 1933; 2nd ed. 1953. Vol. II. Tübingen 1952.)
6. *Das Evangelium des Johannes* (in Meyer's "Critical-Exegetical Commentary on the New Testament", Göttingen 1941; 2nd ed. 1950).
7. *Offenbarung und Heilsgeschehen* (Munich 1941; this contains Two Essays—"Die Frage der natürlichen Offenbarung" and "Neues Testament und Mythologie". It was the second of these that gave rise to the controversy which is the subject of this book).

8. *Theologie des Neuen Testaments* (three volumes with continuous numbering of the pages, Tübingen 1948, 1951, 1953).

9. *Das Urchristentum im Rahmen der antiken Religionen* (Zürich 1949; also in French translation, Paris 1950).

The following are the principal contributors to the controversy on the elimination of the mythological element in the New Testament.

Kerygma und Mythos: Ein theologisches Gespräch; a collection of Essays, edited by Hans Werner Bartsch:

Vol. I. Contributions of Rudolf Bultmann, P. Götz Harbsmeier, P. Friedrich Hochgrebe, Ernst Lohmeyer, Paul Olivier, P. Hermann Sauter, Julius Schniewind, Friedrich K. Schumann, J. B. Soucek, Helmuth Thielicke (Hamburg 1951).

Vol. II. Contributions of Karl Barth, H. W. Bartsch, Fritz Buri, R. Bultmann, Chr. Hartlich and Walter Sachs, W. G. Kümmel, D. A. Oepke, R. Prenter, H. Sauter, E. Stauffer (Hamburg 1952, with a full bibliography of the discussion up to 1952).

Vol. III. Contributions of Karl Jaspers, Kurt Reidemeister, H. W. Bartsch, R. Bultmann, F. Buri (1954).

Vol. IV. Contributions of J. B. Soucek (Prague), L. M. Pakozdy (Debreczen), Ian Henderson (Scotland), Sherman E. Johnson (U.S.A.), R. Gregor Smith (England), Gustav Bröndsted (Denmark), P. Heinz, F. Dressel (Brazil) 1955.

Vol. V. The discussion from the Roman Catholic side. Contributions of K. Adam (Tübingen), Adam Fechter (Freiburg), H. Fries (Tübingen), A. Kolping (Münster), Jérôme Hamer (Paris), R. Schnackenburg (Munich), De Fraine (Louvain), Franser (Louvain) 1955.

Hans Werner Bartsch: *Der gegenwärtige Stand der Entmythologisierungsdebatte* (Hamburg 1955: supplement to Vols. I and II of *Kerygma und Mythos*).

Für und wider die Theologie Bultmanns. Denkschrift der evangelischen theologischen Fakultät der Universität Tübingen (1st and 2nd edd. 1952. A collective judgment of the theological faculty of the University of Tübingen, temperate and well balanced, concerned on the one hand with the liberty of academic teaching, and on the other with the responsibility of the Faculty of Theology in relation to the ecclesiastical community).

G. Bornkamm and W. Klaas: *Mythos und Evangelium: Zum Programm R. Bultmanns* (Munich 1951).

Karl Barth: *Rudolf Bultmann: Ein Versuch ihn zu verstehen* (Zürich-Zollikon, 1952).

Friedrich Gogarten: *Entmythologisierung und Kirche* (Stuttgart 1953).

Karl Jaspers: *Wahrheit und Unheil der Entmythologisierung* in *Schweizerische Theologische Umschau* no. 3/4, 1953.

Rudolf Bultmann: *Zur Frage der Entmythologisierung: Antwort an Karl Jaspers* in *Theologische Zeitschrift*, Basel, March-April, 1954.

J. Bernard: *Bibel und Mythos* (Munich 1954).

H. Fries: *Barth, Bultmann und katholische Theologie* (Munich 1955).

L. Malevez S.J.: *Le message chrétien et le mythe* (Brussels 1954).

Christian Hartlich and Walter Sachs: *Der Ursprung des Mythosbegriffes in der modernen Bibelwissenschaft* (Tübingen 1952).

Günther Backhaus: *Kerygma und Mythos bei David Strauss + Rudolf Bultmann* (Hamburg 1955).

Hans Werner Bartsch: *Kann man von Bultmanns Exegese predigen?* (Hamburg 1955).

Heinrich Ott: *Geschichte und Heilsgeschichte in der Theologie Rudolf Bultmanns* (Tübingen 1955).

The following works of Bultmann have appeared also in English:

No. 3. *Form Criticism.* Chicago-New York 1934.
No. 4. *Jesus*, E. Tr. *Jesus and the Word*, London 1935.
No. 8. *Theology of the New Testament* Vol. I, (tr. Kendrick Grobel, London 1948), Vol. II, (London 1952).
No. 9. *Primitive Christianity* (tr. R. H. Fuller, New York 1956).

No. 5. *Essays, Philosophical and Theological (Glauben und Verstehen* Vol. II. tr. J. C. Grieg), London 1955.
History and Eschatology (Gifford Lectures; Edinburgh, 1957).
In preparation: *The Gospel of John*
　　　　　　　History of the Synoptic Tradition.

Ian Henderson: *History and Myth* (London 1952) is the first general introduction to the whole subject to appear in English.
Kerygma and Myth (tr. R. H. Fuller, London 1953) provides an English version of a number of Essays from *Kerygma und Mythos*, with *An English Appreciation* by Dr. Austin Farrer and a full bibliography of the controversy up to the date of publication.
F. Gogarten: *Demythologising and History* is a translation with some changes and adaptations (by N. Horton Smith, London 1955) of *Entmythologisierung und Kirche.*
J. Macquarrie: *An Existentialist Theology*, 1955, is a comparison of the thought of Bultmann with that of Heidegger.

Index

Aarau, conference at, 84
Adam, Karl, 140 ff., 147
Aeschylus, 116
Aesthetics, 113 f.
Anxiety, dread, 33, 63 ff., 71 f.
Aquinas, Thomas, 142 f.
Arianism, 88
Aristotle, 102, 134
Asceticism, 33, 65
Atheism, 77, 94, 136
Augustine, 71, 75

Bachofen, J. J., 115
Baptism, 7, 29
Barth, Karl, 3, 10, 19, 35, 83, 92, 96, 99 f., 122, 132, 134 f., 141, 147 f.
Bartsch, H. W., 1 f., 138, 147 f.
Bauer, G. L., 112
Bernard, J., 138, 148
Biedermann, 135
Biology, 9, 94
Bornkamm, G., 93, 101, 148
Bousset, W., 14
Buri, F., 140, 147

Calvinism, 140
Chalcedon, council of, 88, 142
Collingwood, R. G., 61
Confessing Church in Germany, 1 f., 108, 110, 115, 146
Couchoud, 125
Covenant, the new, 29, 50
Croce, B., 61
Cullmann, O., 107

De Wette, 113 f.
Death, 7, 9, 37, 40, 63 f.
Decision, challenge to, 14, 19 f., 22, 27, 32 f., 39 f., 43 f., 47 f., 53 f., 59, 74 f., 76 f., 89, 94, 128, 132, 137
"Demythologizing", see Myth
Descartes, 82, 140
Dibelius, M., 16, 121
Dilthey, W., 61, 145
Docetism, 56, 87, 125
Dodd, C. H., 61
Drews, 125
Dualism, 31 f., 36, 50 ff., 59, 103, 145

Ecumenical movement, 85
Eichhorn, J. G., 112
Enlightenment, the, 94, 112 f.

Eschatology, the last things, 9 f., 19, 26 f., 28, 32, 38, 41, 47, 87, 117, 126 f., 137
eschatological event, 22, 33, 39, 43, 47 ff., 55, 77, 84, 88, 125, 129, 132
eschatological existence, 58 ff., 65 ff., 73, 129 ff., 143
Existential, -ism, 12 f., 14, 19 f., 35, 37, 39, 41 f., 44, 54, 61, 62-90, 111, 122, 124, 129, 131 f., 132 ff., 135 f., 140 f.

Faith, 26, 48 ff., 54, 58 f., 61, 64, 66, 74, 81 ff., 89 f., 97, 100, 112, 114, 121, 129, 132 f., 138, 142 f.
faith, the Christian, 3 ff., 20, 67, 74, 94, 101, 113, 117, 122, 124, 130 f., 136 f.
Fechter, A., 141 f., 147
Feuerbach, L., 83, 100, 130
Form-criticism, 16 ff., 19, 21, 24, 105, 120, 126, 142
Fries, H., 113, 138 ff., 147 f.

Gabler, J. P., 112
Gnosticism, 4, 7, 10, 29 ff., 38, 40 f., 45, 51, 53, 55 f., 58, 60 f., 62, 65, 91, 104, 108, 122, 126
Gogarten, F., 148 f.
Gospels, the, 4, 11, 16 ff., 22 ff., 127, 132
Fourth Gospel, 20, 25, 30 f., 45, 50-61, 87, 107 f., 122, 125, 127
Grace, 38 f., 41, 64 f., 69, 72, 81 f., 84, 86 ff., 126
Gressmann, 102
Gunkel, H., 17, 102

Hamer, P. J., 139, 141, 147
Harbsmeier, G., 1, 147
Harnack, A., 13, 106
Hartlich, C., and Sachs, W., 92, 101, 111, 147 f.
Hegel, 113, 134
Heidegger, M., 61, 65, 69, 72, 92, 128, 132, 134 f., 141, 145
Hellenism, 20, 25, 26, 28 ff., 31, 34 f., 104 f., 106, 126
Henderson, I., 147, 149
Herder, 113
Herrmann, W., 83, 128, 130
Heyne, C. G., 112